RESTORATIVE JUSTICE

AND

JUVENILE JUSTICE

SYSTEMS

A Comprehensive Analysis

Dr. Maxwell Shimba

Printed by Shimba Publishing LLC
Printed in the United States of America

TABLE OF CONTENTS

ABSTRACT

The Impact of Restorative Justice on Juvenile Offenders in the Judicial System

Restorative Justice (RJ) represents a transformative shift in addressing criminal behavior, particularly in the juvenile justice system. Unlike traditional punitive approaches, which focus on punishment and deterrence, RJ emphasizes healing, accountability, and reparation between the offender, victim, and the community. This approach is rooted in the belief that crime not only violates laws but also disrupts relationships and harms individuals, communities, and societal bonds. Restorative Justice seeks to repair these harms through inclusive processes that foster dialogue, understanding, and mutually agreed-upon solutions aimed at making amends.

In the context of juvenile offenders, Restorative Justice is especially significant due to the unique developmental and psychological needs of young people. Adolescents are often more susceptible to external influences, prone to impulsivity, and capable of change with the right interventions. The traditional punitive system, which tends to criminalize juvenile behavior, can exacerbate the problem by alienating young offenders from their communities and entrenching them in the criminal justice system. Punitive approaches, such as incarceration or detention, often fail to address the root causes of delinquent behavior, such as trauma, social inequality, or lack of guidance, and can lead to a cycle of recidivism.

Restorative Justice, on the other hand, offers a more constructive alternative. By focusing on accountability, rehabilitation, and reintegration, RJ practices aim to give juveniles the opportunity to understand the impact of their actions, make amends, and restore their place within the community. This process often involves direct or mediated dialogue between the offender and the victim, in which the juvenile is encouraged to take responsibility for their actions, express remorse, and work towards restitution. The inclusion of community members, family, and the victim in these restorative processes creates a more holistic approach to justice, promoting empathy, forgiveness, and personal growth.

Empirical studies and case analyses have demonstrated that Restorative Justice is particularly effective in reducing recidivism among juvenile offenders. Programs such as Victim-Offender Mediation (VOM), Family Group Conferencing (FGC), and Community Restorative Boards have shown that juvenile offenders who participate in RJ processes are less likely to re-offend than those processed through traditional punitive systems. Furthermore, victims who engage in RJ often report higher levels of satisfaction and closure, as the process provides them with a voice, recognition of harm, and, in many cases, compensation or restitution. For juveniles, the opportunity to actively participate in repairing the harm they caused fosters a sense of personal responsibility and moral development that is often absent in traditional justice systems.

Restorative Justice also plays a critical role in promoting rehabilitation. Juvenile offenders are provided with a structured environment where they can learn from their mistakes, address the underlying causes of their behavior, and receive support from both their families and communities. In contrast to punitive measures, which often isolate and stigmatize offenders, RJ practices focus on reintegration, helping juveniles re-establish positive relationships within their community. This holistic approach is crucial for fostering long-term behavioral change and preventing the development of a criminal identity.

From a broader societal perspective, Restorative Justice in juvenile systems also strengthens community cohesion. By involving community members in the justice process, RJ enhances collective responsibility for addressing crime and conflict. Communities are empowered to support the rehabilitation of young offenders and the healing of victims, rather than relying solely on state-driven punitive measures. This participatory model of justice reinforces social bonds and contributes to a more inclusive and resilient society, where individuals are given a second chance to contribute positively to their communities.

The evidence suggests that Restorative Justice can offer a more effective and humane solution to juvenile crime than traditional punitive approaches. By addressing the root causes of delinquent behavior and focusing on rehabilitation and reintegration, RJ has the potential to break the cycle of recidivism that often traps young offenders in the criminal justice system. Moreover, by fostering dialogue, understanding, and mutual respect, RJ promotes healing for both victims and offenders and strengthens the social fabric of communities. In conclusion, the application of Restorative Justice within juvenile justice systems holds great promise in creating a more equitable, just, and compassionate approach to addressing juvenile delinquency, one that prioritizes the well-being of all stakeholders involved.

This thesis will delve into the conceptual foundations, practical applications, and positive outcomes of Restorative Justice in juvenile justice systems, using empirical research, case studies, and theoretical analysis to evaluate its effectiveness. It will explore how RJ practices can reduce recidivism, promote rehabilitation, and foster community cohesion, while also considering the challenges and limitations of implementing Restorative Justice on a wide scale. Ultimately, this study aims to demonstrate that Restorative Justice provides a more suitable and sustainable model for addressing juvenile crime in the 21st century, one that recognizes the potential for growth and change in young offenders while also prioritizing the needs and well-being of victims and communities.

Dr. Maxwell Shimba

DR. MAXWELL SHIMBA

CHAPTER 01

INTRODUCTION

1.1 Background of the Study

The traditional criminal justice system, particularly in Western societies, has historically been rooted in a retributive philosophy that emphasizes punishment as the primary response to crime. This approach is largely focused on assigning blame to the offender, determining guilt, and subsequently imposing penalties, typically in the form of incarceration or other punitive measures. The underlying assumption of this model is that punishment serves as a deterrent to future crimes, both for the individual offender and society at large. However, over time, concerns have arisen regarding the effectiveness of this model, especially when applied to juvenile offenders.

Punitive justice for juveniles often fails to consider the developmental and psychological differences between children and adults. Juveniles are not simply miniature adults;

their cognitive and emotional development is ongoing, and their behavior is often influenced by factors such as immaturity, lack of foresight, peer pressure, and challenging socio-economic or familial environments. As a result, their involvement in criminal behavior is frequently tied to a lack of understanding of the long-term consequences of their actions rather than a deeply ingrained criminal mindset. Moreover, adolescents are more amenable to rehabilitation and behavior modification compared to adults, as they are still in a critical phase of identity formation and character development.

Despite these factors, juvenile offenders in many countries are often subjected to the same punitive measures as adult offenders, including detention, incarceration, and criminal records. These punitive responses can have long-lasting and damaging effects on young offenders. Research has shown that exposing juveniles to harsh, punitive environments such as detention centers or correctional facilities can exacerbate negative behaviors, leading to higher rates of recidivism. Rather than rehabilitating these young individuals, such punitive measures often stigmatize and alienate them from their communities, reinforcing criminal identities and cycles of offending.

In contrast, Restorative Justice (RJ) offers an alternative framework that shifts the focus from punishment to healing and repair. Restorative Justice is grounded in the understanding that crime is not just a violation of the law, but a harm done to individuals, relationships, and communities. Therefore, RJ seeks to address these harms through processes that encourage accountability, empathy, and reconciliation. This approach is particularly beneficial for juvenile offenders, as it provides them with opportunities to learn from their mistakes, make amends, and develop a sense of responsibility and moral growth. RJ emphasizes the importance of reintegrating offenders back into their communities rather than ostracizing them, thus preventing the social alienation that can lead to further criminal behavior.

Restorative Justice practices, such as Victim-Offender Mediation (VOM), Family Group Conferencing (FGC), and Restorative Circles, are designed to create a space where the juvenile offender, the victim, and community members can come together to discuss the offense and its impacts. In this process, the offender is encouraged to take responsibility for their actions, understand the harm caused, and actively work towards repairing the damage. This reparative action may include apologizing, compensating the victim, or performing community service. For victims, this process often provides a sense of closure and empowerment, as they are given a platform to express their feelings and needs, which is often absent in traditional justice proceedings.

For juvenile offenders, Restorative Justice provides a path towards personal development and reintegration into society. By fostering a deeper understanding of the consequences of their actions and encouraging them to take active steps towards making amends, RJ helps juveniles develop a stronger sense of empathy and accountability. This personal growth can have long-term positive effects, as it equips young offenders with the skills and awareness needed to avoid future criminal behavior. Moreover, RJ often involves the offender's family and community, which helps to create a supportive network that can guide the young individual back onto a constructive path.

Another critical aspect of Restorative Justice for juveniles is the emphasis on education and rehabilitation. Traditional punitive measures, such as incarceration, often fail to address the underlying causes of juvenile offending, such as trauma, poverty, substance abuse, or educational challenges. In contrast, RJ processes frequently involve tailored rehabilitation programs that address these root causes. These programs may include counseling, mentoring, substance abuse treatment, and educational support, all of which are designed to help the juvenile build a foundation for a successful, law-abiding future.

Furthermore, Restorative Justice aligns with contemporary understandings of child development and juvenile delinquency. The scientific community increasingly recognizes that the adolescent brain is still developing, particularly in areas related to decision-making, impulse control, and empathy. This developmental perspective supports the notion that juveniles are capable of significant change and rehabilitation if given the right opportunities. Restorative Justice, by focusing on rehabilitation rather than punishment, offers an approach that aligns with this understanding of adolescent development, acknowledging that young offenders are still in the process of forming their identities and moral compasses.

Internationally, many juvenile justice systems have begun to integrate Restorative Justice practices, recognizing their potential to address the limitations of traditional punitive models. Countries such as New Zealand, Canada, and Norway have been pioneers in adopting RJ practices, particularly in their juvenile justice systems. For example, New Zealand's use of Family Group Conferencing as a standard response to juvenile crime has been widely recognized as a model for other nations. This approach has resulted in lower recidivism rates and higher levels of satisfaction among victims, offenders, and communities.

In conclusion, the rise of Restorative Justice represents a paradigm shift in how societies view and respond to juvenile crime. By focusing on healing, accountability, and reintegration, RJ offers a more humane and constructive alternative to punitive justice. It recognizes the developmental needs of juvenile offenders and provides them with opportunities for growth, rehabilitation, and reintegration. This study aims to explore the various dimensions of Restorative Justice in juvenile systems, assessing its effectiveness in promoting long-term positive outcomes for offenders, victims, and society as a whole.

1.2 Research Objectives

The primary objective of this thesis is to critically assess the application and effectiveness of Restorative Justice (RJ) within juvenile justice systems. Restorative Justice represents a shift from traditional punitive models toward approaches that prioritize healing, accountability, and reconciliation, particularly focusing on young offenders who are in developmental stages. The aim is to explore how RJ operates as a viable alternative to punitive responses, addressing the complex needs of juveniles, victims, and communities in the justice process. By doing so, the research seeks to demonstrate how RJ not only aids in rehabilitating juvenile offenders but also contributes to the overall well-being and safety of society. To meet this goal, the research will be guided by several secondary objectives, which align closely with the key research questions.

1.2.1 Analyzing the Effectiveness of Restorative Justice in Reducing Recidivism Among Juvenile Offenders

One of the most pressing concerns in juvenile justice is the high rate of recidivism—where offenders, after serving punitive sentences, return to criminal behavior. This objective seeks to analyze how RJ can serve as an intervention that reduces these reoffending rates by addressing the root causes of juvenile crime and offering a rehabilitative rather than purely punitive response. Juvenile offenders often commit crimes due to social, psychological, or economic factors, such as peer influence, family breakdown, trauma, or lack of guidance. Punitive systems often fail to address these underlying issues, whereas RJ approaches provide juveniles with the opportunity to take responsibility for their actions and make reparations, fostering personal growth and behavioral change.

To accomplish this objective, the research will focus on empirical studies, longitudinal research, and case studies that document recidivism rates in jurisdictions that have implemented RJ practices within juvenile systems. By comparing these data with recidivism rates in traditional punitive systems, the research will determine whether RJ is a more effective long-term solution for reducing reoffending among juvenile populations. Additionally, the research will examine the mechanisms within RJ that contribute to this reduction, such as offender accountability, victim-offender dialogue, and community support systems.

1.2.2 Exploring the Theoretical Foundations and Principles that Support Restorative Justice

The success and credibility of any justice system, particularly Restorative Justice, lie in its underlying principles and theoretical framework. This objective focuses on providing a thorough exploration of the theoretical foundations that give legitimacy and structure to RJ. By examining theories from criminology, sociology, psychology, and conflict resolution, this study will contextualize how RJ emerged as a response to the shortcomings of retributive justice models.

Key theoretical perspectives such as Social Constructivism, which sees crime as a breakdown in social relationships, and Communitarian Theory, which emphasizes the role of community in addressing harm, will be analyzed.

Additionally, Conflict Resolution Theory will be discussed, as it provides insights into how RJ facilitates dialogue and reconciliation between offenders, victims, and communities.

This objective is designed to answer fundamental research questions, such as: What are the key principles that underpin Restorative Justice? How does RJ differ from traditional justice models, particularly in the way it addresses crime, accountability, and community relationships? By addressing these questions, the research will demonstrate why RJ is particularly well-suited for application within juvenile justice systems, where young offenders are still in the process of moral and social development.

1.2.3 Investigating the Practical Application of Restorative Justice Through Case Studies and Empirical Research

While understanding the theoretical underpinnings of RJ is crucial, its practical application is equally important to assess how RJ operates on the ground, especially in juvenile justice systems. This objective aims to explore how RJ is implemented in different jurisdictions and what outcomes have been observed in these contexts. The research will utilize case studies from countries such as New Zealand, Canada, the United States, and other nations that have embraced RJ practices for juveniles. These case studies will provide real-world examples of how RJ functions in practice, detailing specific processes like Victim-Offender Mediation (VOM), Family Group Conferencing (FGC), and Restorative Circles.

For example, in New Zealand, the Family Group Conferencing model is used as an alternative to formal court proceedings for juvenile offenders. This study will investigate how such models operate, the extent of community involvement, the nature of agreements reached between offenders and victims, and the impact on recidivism and rehabilitation. By analyzing these case studies, this research will evaluate the effectiveness of RJ in different socio-cultural and legal environments, providing a nuanced understanding of its practical outcomes.

Furthermore, the research will incorporate empirical studies that provide quantitative data on RJ's impact, such as reductions in juvenile recidivism, victim satisfaction rates, and the long-term social reintegration of offenders. These studies will be vital for answering research questions like: How is Restorative Justice practically applied in different juvenile systems? What measurable outcomes arise from its implementation?

1.2.4 Evaluating the Role of Community, Victims, and Juvenile Offenders in the Restorative Process

Restorative Justice is unique in its emphasis on the active involvement of all stakeholders in the justice process, including the offender, the victim, and the community. This objective seeks to explore the distinct roles each of these parties plays in RJ practices, particularly in the context of juvenile justice.

For the juvenile offender, RJ represents a chance to take responsibility for their actions in a constructive way. Instead of being passively subjected to punishment, the offender is encouraged to engage with the victim, understand the harm caused, and work towards making amends. The research will evaluate how this participatory role contributes to the offender's moral development and future behavior, as well as how RJ helps juveniles reintegrate into their communities post-offense.

For victims, RJ offers an opportunity to be heard and to receive direct restitution, whether through an apology, financial compensation, or community service. Traditional justice systems often marginalize the victim's voice, focusing instead on state-imposed punishment. This research will evaluate how victim participation in RJ can lead to a greater sense of justice and closure, as well as increased satisfaction with the outcome of the process.

Finally, for the community, RJ fosters a sense of collective responsibility for both preventing crime and supporting the reintegration of offenders. Communities play a critical role in monitoring agreements made through RJ processes and offering the support needed to rehabilitate the juvenile offender. This objective will analyze how community involvement strengthens social bonds and prevents further criminal behavior, answering research questions such as: How do victims, offenders, and the community engage in Restorative Justice processes? What is the role of community support in the success of RJ outcomes for juveniles?

By aligning these detailed objectives with the research questions, this thesis aims to provide a comprehensive examination of Restorative Justice in juvenile justice systems. The focus will not only be on the conceptual and theoretical underpinnings of RJ but also on its practical application and measurable outcomes. Through a thorough analysis of case studies, empirical data, and the roles of key stakeholders, this research seeks to demonstrate how RJ can serve as an effective, humane, and rehabilitative alternative to punitive juvenile justice systems.

1.3 Research Questions

The research questions guide the core inquiry of this thesis, focusing on the theoretical, practical, and social dimensions of Restorative Justice (RJ) in juvenile justice systems. Each question seeks to address a specific aspect of RJ's application, effectiveness, and impact on key stakeholders, particularly juvenile offenders, victims, and communities.

1.3.1 What Are the Key Principles and Theoretical Frameworks That Underpin Restorative Justice?

This question seeks to explore the foundational principles and theories that shape Restorative Justice as a distinctive model within the broader context of criminal justice. Understanding these principles is critical for evaluating why RJ is often seen as a more appropriate and effective approach for juvenile offenders compared to traditional punitive justice systems. The question will explore:

- The core values of RJ, such as accountability, healing, reparation, and community participation.

- Theoretical frameworks that support RJ, including Social Constructivism, which views crime as a disruption of relationships rather than simply a violation of the law; Conflict Resolution Theory, which emphasizes dialogue and mutual understanding; and Communitarian Theory, which underscores the role of community in addressing crime and reintegrating offenders.

- Restorative Justice's contrast with retributive justice, particularly in its approach to dealing with juvenile offenders, emphasizing rehabilitation over punishment.

By answering this question, the research will provide a comprehensive understanding of the philosophical and theoretical foundations that make RJ a compelling alternative for addressing juvenile crime.

1.3.2 How Is Restorative Justice Applied Within the Context of Juvenile Justice Systems?

This question focuses on the practical application of Restorative Justice in juvenile justice systems. RJ practices vary across different jurisdictions, with models such as Victim-Offender Mediation (VOM), Family Group Conferencing (FGC), and Restorative Circles being used to address juvenile offenses. This question seeks to:

- Examine how RJ is implemented in different legal systems and cultural contexts, with particular emphasis on countries like New Zealand, Canada, and the United States, where RJ practices have been integrated into juvenile justice.

- Analyze different RJ models and processes, such as mediation, conferencing, and community restorative boards, and how they function in practice to bring offenders, victims, and communities together.

- Investigate the involvement of stakeholders, including the juvenile offender, the victim, family members, and the broader community, in the RJ process.

By addressing this question, the research will evaluate how RJ has been adapted and implemented specifically within juvenile justice systems, highlighting the practical steps taken to ensure the success of these programs.

1.3.3 What Are the Measurable Outcomes of Implementing Restorative Justice Practices on Juvenile Recidivism?

A crucial aspect of evaluating Restorative Justice is its effectiveness in reducing recidivism rates among juvenile offenders. This question aims to measure the tangible impact of RJ interventions on the likelihood of reoffending. Specifically, the research will:

- Analyze empirical data on recidivism rates among juveniles who have participated in RJ programs compared to those processed through traditional punitive systems.

- Identify the factors within RJ that contribute to the reduction of recidivism, such as the emphasis on offender accountability, the reparative nature of the agreements reached, and the support systems put in place for reintegration.

- Examine long-term outcomes for juvenile offenders who have engaged in RJ, assessing whether they experience sustained rehabilitation and successful reintegration into society.

This question will be answered through the analysis of case studies and longitudinal research that tracks the effectiveness of RJ programs in preventing reoffending, offering a data-driven perspective on RJ's capacity to address juvenile crime.

1.3.4 How Do Victims and Communities Perceive and Engage in the Restorative Process with Juvenile Offenders?

Restorative Justice is unique in its focus on the needs and involvement of victims and communities, in addition to the offender. This question aims to explore the perceptions and experiences of these key stakeholders in RJ processes. The research will:

- Examine the satisfaction levels of victims who participate in RJ processes, compared to traditional justice systems, where their role is often limited. The research will look into how RJ provides victims with a voice and an opportunity for closure.

- Evaluate the role of the community in supporting both the victim and the juvenile offender. This includes the community's involvement in decision-making, monitoring restitution agreements, and facilitating the offender's reintegration.

- Analyze the outcomes for victims, such as emotional healing, restitution, and empowerment, through their active involvement in RJ.

- Assess community perceptions of RJ and how community members perceive the effectiveness of the process in maintaining social order, preventing future crime, and fostering communal ties.

By addressing this question, the research will provide insights into how Restorative Justice fosters positive engagement among victims and communities, contributing to its overall success and sustainability within juvenile justice systems.

Each of these research questions aligns with the overall objectives of the thesis, providing a comprehensive framework for examining Restorative Justice in juvenile systems. The study will delve into both the theoretical foundations and practical applications of RJ, while also evaluating its measurable outcomes and impact on key stakeholders.

1.4 Methodology

This research adopts a mixed-methods approach, combining both qualitative and quantitative research methodologies to provide a comprehensive understanding of the application and effectiveness of Restorative Justice (RJ) in juvenile justice systems. The mixed-methods approach allows for a robust analysis of both theoretical perspectives and empirical data, enabling the study to assess the nuanced dimensions of RJ and its real-world impacts on juvenile offenders, victims, and communities. The approach also enhances the reliability and validity of the findings by triangulating data from various sources.

1.4.1 Qualitative Research Methods

Literature Review

The qualitative aspect of this study involves a thorough review of literature to establish a theoretical foundation for Restorative Justice in juvenile justice systems. This literature review will encompass academic journals, books, governmental reports, and research papers that provide insights into RJ's theoretical frameworks, guiding principles, and practical application. The following elements will be explored in the literature review:

- Historical development of Restorative Justice in both adult and juvenile justice systems.

- Key theoretical perspectives underpinning RJ, such as Social Constructivism, Conflict Resolution Theory, and Communitarian Theory.

- Global perspectives on RJ, focusing on countries like New Zealand, Canada, and the United States, which have implemented RJ practices in their juvenile justice systems.

The literature review will help contextualize Restorative Justice as a concept, its evolution over time, and its relevance to modern judicial systems.

Case Studies

The qualitative component will also include an analysis of case studies from jurisdictions that have successfully implemented RJ practices for juveniles. These case studies provide real-world examples of how Restorative Justice operates, the challenges encountered, and the outcomes achieved. For instance, the research will examine:

- New Zealand's Family Group Conferencing model, which is considered a global leader in RJ practices within juvenile justice.

- Minnesota's Restorative Justice programs for juveniles, focusing on their impact on recidivism rates and victim satisfaction.

\- Canada's use of Victim-Offender Mediation and the success of RJ in reducing recidivism and fostering community participation.

These case studies will provide detailed insights into how RJ models are implemented in practice and will offer lessons that can be applied in today's judicial systems.

Interviews with Practitioners

The research will also involve conducting interviews with key practitioners in the field of Restorative Justice, including mediators, juvenile justice officers, legal professionals, and community leaders. These interviews will provide firsthand insights into:

\- The practical challenges of implementing RJ in juvenile systems.

\- Perceptions of effectiveness from professionals working directly with juvenile offenders and victims.

\- Lessons learned from RJ practices and suggestions for improving the system.

Interviews with practitioners will add depth to the qualitative analysis by highlighting practical experiences, challenges, and recommendations for further improvement.

1.4.2 Quantitative Research Methods

Secondary Data Analysis

To assess the effectiveness of Restorative Justice, particularly in terms of reducing recidivism among juveniles, the quantitative aspect of this research will focus on secondary data analysis. Secondary data, including statistical reports and longitudinal studies from countries that have adopted RJ practices in their juvenile justice systems, will be analyzed to provide measurable outcomes. Specifically, the research will focus on:

- Recidivism rates: Data on juvenile reoffending rates in RJ programs compared to those in traditional punitive systems will be analyzed. This will include longitudinal studies that track offenders over time.

- Victim satisfaction surveys: Quantitative data from surveys conducted with victims involved in RJ processes will be examined to measure victim satisfaction, restitution fulfillment, and perceptions of justice.

- Community involvement metrics: The research will look at how communities participate in RJ programs, including levels of community support and involvement in mediation, conferencing, and restorative boards.

The analysis of secondary data will help answer key research questions regarding the measurable impact of RJ on juvenile recidivism and the perceptions of stakeholders.

Comparative Analysis

A comparative analysis of RJ programs across different jurisdictions will also be conducted. By comparing data from multiple countries (such as New Zealand, the United States, and Canada), this analysis will assess:

- Differences in recidivism rates between RJ-based juvenile justice systems and traditional punitive systems.

- Effectiveness of different RJ models (e.g., Family Group Conferencing, Victim-Offender Mediation) in achieving positive outcomes for both juveniles and victims.

- Socioeconomic factors that may influence the success of RJ programs, such as the level of community support, availability of resources, and cultural attitudes towards rehabilitation and punishment.

The comparative analysis will offer insights into how various RJ models can be adapted and applied within contemporary judicial systems in different regions.

1.4.3 Application of Methodologies to Today's Judicial System

The methodologies used in this study provide important insights and data that can be directly applied to contemporary judicial systems, especially in societies grappling with high juvenile crime rates and overburdened punitive systems. In today's context, the following applications of Restorative Justice can be derived from the research methodologies:

- Policy Development: By utilizing the findings from literature reviews and case studies, policymakers can craft juvenile justice reforms that integrate RJ practices as a core component, focusing on rehabilitation rather than punishment.

- Recidivism Reduction Programs: Data from secondary sources on the effectiveness of RJ in reducing recidivism can inform the development of targeted intervention programs in juvenile detention centers, schools, and community organizations.

- Training for RJ Practitioners: Interviews with RJ practitioners can highlight the specific skills and training required for mediators, justice officers, and community leaders to effectively implement RJ programs.

- Community Engagement Models: The analysis of case studies and community involvement metrics can inform strategies to enhance community participation in the justice process, ensuring that community members are actively engaged in reintegrating juvenile offenders.

- Victim Support Services: Quantitative data on victim satisfaction can be used to enhance victim support services within RJ programs, ensuring that victims feel heard, respected, and compensated.

1.4.4 Data Collection Tools and Ethical Considerations

Data will be collected through various tools, including:

- Interviews and surveys with RJ practitioners, victims, and juvenile offenders.

- Data collection from government reports and RJ program statistics.

- Literature databases to gather peer-reviewed articles, case studies, and theoretical perspectives.

Ethical considerations will include maintaining the confidentiality of interview participants, obtaining informed consent, and ensuring that data collection does not harm vulnerable populations, particularly juvenile offenders and victims involved in RJ processes.

By utilizing this mixed-methods approach, this study will provide a comprehensive evaluation of Restorative Justice in juvenile systems. The integration of qualitative and quantitative research allows for a detailed understanding of both the theoretical and practical implications of RJ, offering valuable insights that can be applied to modern judicial reforms aimed at rehabilitating juvenile offenders.

CHAPTER 02

THEORETICAL FRAMEWORK OF RESTORATIVE JUSTICE

2.1 Defining Restorative Justice

Restorative Justice (RJ) is a justice paradigm that seeks to address the harm caused by criminal behavior through inclusive processes that involve the offender, the victim, and the broader community. Unlike traditional retributive justice, which emphasizes punishment as a response to wrongdoing, RJ focuses on healing the relationships and individuals affected by the crime. The primary goal of RJ is to repair the damage caused by the offense, restore relationships, and reintegrate the offender into society in a constructive manner.

At its core, RJ is grounded in principles of accountability, empathy, and reparation. It shifts the focus from merely punishing the offender to understanding the root causes of the offense, fostering personal responsibility, and promoting meaningful dialogue among the affected parties. This approach seeks to resolve the conflict created by the offense, address the needs of both the victim and the offender, and ultimately prevent future harm by promoting behavioral change. RJ methods such as victim-offender mediation, family group conferencing, and community restorative circles encourage active participation and collaborative problem-solving.

Restorative Justice and Juvenile Offenders

In the context of juvenile offenders, Restorative Justice takes on a particularly significant role. Juveniles, due to their developmental stage, are seen as more malleable and capable of reform than adult offenders. Their involvement in criminal activities is often a result of a combination of factors such as immaturity, peer pressure, social inequalities, or adverse childhood experiences. The punitive measures typically imposed by traditional justice systems can have detrimental effects on juvenile offenders, such as stigmatization, social isolation, and further entrenchment in criminal behavior.

Restorative Justice, in contrast, recognizes the unique needs and circumstances of juveniles. It provides them with opportunities for personal growth, reflection, and rehabilitation rather than subjecting them to the punitive and adversarial processes that characterize conventional justice systems. RJ practices enable juvenile offenders to take responsibility for their actions in a way that promotes understanding of the harm caused and encourages behavioral change.

Key elements of RJ for juveniles include:

- Accountability: Juveniles are encouraged to understand the consequences of their actions on victims and the community. They actively participate in making amends, which may involve direct dialogue with the victim or participation in restitution processes such as community service.

- Empathy and Emotional Learning: Through the restorative process, juvenile offenders are guided to develop empathy for the victim and recognize the human impact of their actions. This emotional learning is critical in fostering moral and social development.

- Rehabilitation and Reintegration: Unlike punitive approaches that often isolate young offenders, RJ prioritizes rehabilitation and reintegration. It works to ensure that juveniles are not alienated from society but instead are supported in their efforts to reform and reintegrate as responsible community members.

- Victim-Centered Approach: RJ also empowers victims by providing them with a voice in the justice process. Victims are not sidelined, as they often are in traditional systems, but are central to the resolution process. This can offer them a sense of closure and healing.

By focusing on repair rather than retribution, Restorative Justice encourages juvenile offenders to take responsibility for their behavior in ways that contribute to their rehabilitation. RJ acknowledges the potential for growth and change in young people and provides a framework for addressing criminal behavior without subjecting them to the potentially harmful effects of a purely punitive system.

Restorative Justice as a Response to Juvenile Crime

Juvenile crime, while often less serious in nature than adult crime, can have profound consequences for the individuals involved and the community at large. Traditional punitive responses, such as incarceration or formal criminal records, often fail to address the underlying causes of juvenile offending. Furthermore, punitive measures can disproportionately affect vulnerable or marginalized youth, exacerbating social inequalities and reinforcing cycles of disadvantage and crime.

Restorative Justice offers an alternative that seeks to address the root causes of juvenile offending while providing pathways to rehabilitation. RJ is particularly relevant for juvenile offenders because it is centered on the recognition that young people are still in the process of developing their moral and social identities. Unlike punitive approaches that may harden or alienate young offenders, RJ processes encourage reflection, learning, and personal growth.

By involving offenders, victims, and the community, RJ promotes a holistic response to crime. Juvenile offenders are encouraged to take part in family group conferencing or victim-offender mediation, where they engage directly with their victims and work together to develop solutions to repair the harm caused. This process not only provides victims with a platform to express their feelings and needs but also helps offenders understand the impact of their actions and how they can make amends.

RJ also emphasizes the importance of community involvement in the justice process. Juveniles are often part of larger social networks, including families, schools, and communities, all of which can play a crucial role in preventing further offending. By involving these networks in the restorative process, RJ provides a supportive framework that helps juveniles reintegrate into society and reduces the likelihood of future criminal behavior.

The Impact of Restorative Justice on Juvenile Recidivism

A key objective of juvenile justice systems is to prevent reoffending. Studies have shown that punitive measures, such as incarceration, often fail to deter juveniles from engaging in further criminal activity. In many cases, punitive measures can increase the likelihood of recidivism, as juveniles who are exposed to the criminal justice system may become more isolated from positive social influences and more deeply entrenched in criminal subcultures.

Restorative Justice has proven to be an effective tool in reducing recidivism among juvenile offenders. By focusing on rehabilitation and the reintegration of the offender into the community, RJ provides juveniles with the opportunity to learn from their mistakes and make positive changes. RJ practices help juveniles develop social and emotional skills, such as empathy, self-regulation, and problem-solving, which are critical for reducing the risk of future criminal behavior.

Empirical studies demonstrate that juvenile offenders who participate in RJ programs are less likely to reoffend than those processed through traditional punitive systems. This reduction in recidivism can be attributed to the fact that RJ addresses the underlying causes of juvenile crime, such as family dysfunction, peer pressure, and lack of guidance, and provides offenders with the tools and support they need to avoid future involvement in crime.

Conclusion

Restorative Justice offers a forward-thinking, rehabilitative approach to juvenile crime that contrasts with the punitive responses of traditional justice systems. By focusing on accountability, emotional learning, and community reintegration, RJ provides juvenile offenders with the opportunity to repair the harm caused by their actions while fostering personal growth and development. Involving victims and the community in the justice process ensures that all stakeholders have a voice, leading to outcomes that promote healing and reconciliation. This makes Restorative Justice a powerful and effective model for addressing juvenile crime in a way that supports both offender rehabilitation and community well-being.

2.2 Historical Development of Restorative Justice

The concept of Restorative Justice (RJ), though widely recognized in contemporary legal systems, has deep historical roots in indigenous justice practices that emphasized healing, reconciliation, and community involvement rather than punishment. Indigenous cultures worldwide have long recognized that crime is not just a violation of laws but a disruption to relationships and social harmony. The historical development of RJ reflects a return to these time-honored principles of justice, particularly in response to the growing dissatisfaction with punitive justice systems in the modern era. Juvenile justice, in particular, has played a significant role in the resurgence of RJ, as societies have come to recognize the need for a more rehabilitative and constructive approach to dealing with young offenders.

Indigenous Roots of Restorative Justice

The origins of RJ can be traced back to the justice practices of indigenous communities across the world, where the emphasis was on restoring balance and repairing harm rather than focusing solely on punishing the offender. These practices were grounded in a belief that crime harms not only the victim but also the entire community, and thus the community must be involved in the process of healing and resolution.

- Maori in New Zealand: The Maori people of New Zealand practiced a form of justice known as whakapapa, where the offender was brought together with the victim, their families, and the wider community to discuss the harm caused and determine how to repair it. This communal approach was focused on healing and reintegrating the offender back into the community, rather than ostracizing them. Family Group Conferencing, a central practice in modern RJ, is heavily inspired by these Maori traditions and has become a cornerstone of New Zealand's juvenile justice system.

- First Nations in Canada: Many First Nations communities in Canada practiced justice through circle sentencing, where the offender, victim, and community members would sit in a circle and engage in dialogue about the crime. The aim was to come to a consensus on how the offender could make amends and restore harmony to the community. This process was deeply rooted in the belief that crime affected the entire community and that collective action was necessary to repair the harm. Today, circle sentencing is used in both adult and juvenile RJ processes in Canada.

- Native American Tribes: Similar practices existed among Native American tribes in the United States, where community-based methods of conflict resolution focused on restoring harmony rather than meting out punishment. These practices recognized the interconnectedness of individuals within the community and the need for collective healing after a crime.

The key principles of these indigenous practices—community involvement, healing, and reintegration—are central to modern Restorative Justice. They stand in stark contrast to the retributive justice systems that emerged in Europe and became the dominant model in Western societies, where the state took over the role of punishing offenders, often with little regard for the needs of the victim or the community.

Emergence of Restorative Justice in Modern Legal Systems

In the modern context, Restorative Justice gained prominence in the 1970s as a response to the growing dissatisfaction with punitive justice systems. Throughout much of the 20th century, criminal justice systems in many parts of the world were based on retributive models that focused on punishment and deterrence. However, this approach was increasingly seen as ineffective, particularly in the context of juvenile justice. High rates of recidivism, overcrowded prisons, and the failure to rehabilitate offenders led to calls for alternatives that focused on restoration rather than retribution.

Several key developments in the 1970s marked the re-emergence of RJ:

- Victim-Offender Mediation (VOM): One of the earliest modern RJ practices was Victim-Offender Mediation, which began in Canada and the United States in the 1970s. In this process, the offender and victim meet in a mediated session to discuss the crime, its impact, and how the offender can make amends. This approach emphasized direct accountability and dialogue between the offender and the victim, with the goal of repairing the harm done.

- Family Group Conferencing (FGC): Inspired by Maori traditions, Family Group Conferencing was introduced in New Zealand in the 1980s as a response to the failure of the juvenile justice system to address the needs of young offenders and their communities. FGC brought together the juvenile offender, the victim, their families, and community members in a meeting to discuss the offense and agree on a plan for making amends. This model was highly successful and became a key feature of New Zealand's juvenile justice system, eventually being adopted by other countries.

- Circle Sentencing: Drawing on the practices of First Nations in Canada, circle sentencing was introduced into the Canadian justice system in the 1990s. This process involved not only the offender and victim but also the wider community, in a dialogue aimed at finding a restorative solution to the crime. Circle sentencing became particularly prominent in juvenile cases, as it provided a way for young offenders to take responsibility for their actions in a supportive, non-punitive environment.

These developments marked the beginning of a broader movement toward RJ in criminal justice systems around the world. By the late 20th century, RJ was being increasingly recognized as a viable alternative to punitive justice, especially for juveniles.

The Role of Juvenile Justice in the Development of Restorative Justice

Juvenile justice systems have played a central role in the adoption and evolution of Restorative Justice. Historically, juveniles were often treated in the same way as adult offenders, subjected to harsh punishments that failed to account for their developmental needs and potential for rehabilitation. However, over time, it became clear that punitive responses were not only ineffective for juveniles but also often harmful. Incarcerating young offenders, particularly in environments with older, more hardened criminals, led to negative outcomes such as recidivism, trauma, and the entrenchment of criminal behavior.

The failures of traditional juvenile justice systems created a demand for alternatives that could better address the needs of young offenders. Restorative Justice emerged as a powerful solution, offering a way to hold juveniles accountable while also providing opportunities for rehabilitation and reintegration. The following factors explain why RJ became especially relevant in juvenile justice:

- Developmental Considerations: Juveniles are still in the process of developing cognitively, emotionally, and socially. Their offending behavior is often a result of immaturity, poor decision-making, or external influences such as peer pressure or family dysfunction. Restorative Justice recognizes these developmental factors and provides juveniles with a process that promotes learning, accountability, and emotional growth, rather than simply punishing them.

- Potential for Rehabilitation: Unlike adults, juveniles are generally more capable of change. Restorative Justice processes are designed to encourage self-reflection and personal growth, helping young offenders understand the consequences of their actions and make amends. This rehabilitative focus makes RJ especially well-suited for addressing juvenile crime.

- Community and Family Involvement: Juveniles are often deeply embedded in their family and community structures, which play a critical role in their development. RJ practices, such as Family Group Conferencing and circle sentencing, actively involve the family and community in the justice process, helping to support the juvenile offender's rehabilitation and reintegration. This community-oriented approach is particularly effective in preventing further offending and supporting positive development.

- Lower Recidivism Rates: Empirical studies have shown that Restorative Justice is more effective than punitive measures in reducing recidivism among juvenile offenders. By focusing on repairing harm and providing support, RJ helps to break the cycle of reoffending, allowing juveniles to reintegrate into society as responsible individuals.

Conclusion

The historical development of Restorative Justice is deeply rooted in indigenous traditions of communal healing and reconciliation, where crime was seen as a disruption to relationships that needed to be repaired. In the modern era, RJ emerged as a response to the failures of punitive justice systems, particularly in juvenile justice, where traditional approaches often did more harm than good. Juveniles, with their unique developmental needs and potential for rehabilitation, have been central to the evolution of RJ, which offers a more compassionate, constructive, and effective approach to addressing youth crime. Through processes such as mediation, conferencing, and community involvement, RJ has proven to be a powerful tool for reducing recidivism and promoting positive outcomes for both young offenders and society.

2.3 Key Principles of Restorative Justice

Restorative Justice (RJ) is guided by a set of foundational principles that shape its approach to addressing crime and the harm it causes. These principles provide the philosophical framework for RJ processes and practices, focusing on healing, responsibility, and community engagement rather than punishment. RJ's core principles — accountability, reparation, inclusion, and reintegration — are particularly relevant when applied to juvenile offenders, offering a constructive pathway toward rehabilitation and reconciliation. Each principle reflects the values that underpin RJ and its commitment to repairing harm and preventing further criminal behavior.

2.3.1 Accountability

Accountability is at the heart of Restorative Justice. Unlike punitive justice systems, which often focus on punishing the offender without necessarily fostering understanding or responsibility, RJ emphasizes that offenders must take responsibility for their actions. Accountability in RJ goes beyond admitting guilt; it requires the offender to fully comprehend the impact of their behavior on the victim, the community, and their own life.

For juvenile offenders, this principle is crucial for fostering personal growth and moral development. Adolescents are often still learning to navigate complex social relationships and may not fully understand the consequences of their actions. In RJ processes, juvenile offenders are encouraged to engage directly with the harm they have caused, often through dialogue with the victim or participation in a community setting. This engagement helps them recognize the emotional, financial, and social impacts of their behavior and take responsibility for repairing the damage.

- Personal Responsibility: Juveniles are asked to reflect on their actions and accept responsibility in a constructive manner. This reflection helps them internalize the importance of personal accountability and the role they play in maintaining social harmony.

- Active Participation: Unlike in traditional justice systems, where offenders are often passive recipients of punishment, RJ requires the offender to actively participate in the process of making amends. This active engagement promotes accountability in a more meaningful way.

By holding juvenile offenders accountable in a supportive and educational environment, RJ helps them develop the skills and awareness necessary to avoid future offending, creating a foundation for long-term behavioral change.

2.3.2 Reparation

The principle of reparation focuses on repairing the harm caused by criminal behavior. In Restorative Justice, the goal is not only to address the legal implications of the offense but also to heal the emotional and relational damage caused to the victim, the community, and the offender. Reparation is typically achieved through restitution, community service, or other restorative actions agreed upon by the victim, offender, and community.

Reparation is particularly impactful in juvenile justice settings, where offenders are often able to make tangible efforts to right their wrongs. The concept of reparation encourages offenders to confront the consequences of their actions and take meaningful steps to make amends. For juvenile offenders, reparation may take many forms, including:

- Restitution: Juvenile offenders may be asked to compensate victims for financial losses or damages incurred as a result of their actions. This can include monetary payments, the return of stolen goods, or other forms of compensation.

- Community Service: In cases where financial restitution is not possible or appropriate, juvenile offenders may engage in community service projects that benefit the wider community. This serves both as a way to repay the harm and to foster a sense of civic responsibility.

- Apology and Acknowledgment: Sometimes, the most significant form of reparation comes in the form of a sincere apology and acknowledgment of the harm caused. Through victim-offender dialogues, juveniles can offer personal apologies, which can help victims heal and provide offenders with a deeper understanding of the emotional impacts of their actions.

Reparation in RJ is not solely about restoring material losses but also about rebuilding trust and relationships. Juveniles are given the opportunity to demonstrate that they are committed to making things right, which contributes to their rehabilitation and reintegration into society.

2.3.3 Inclusion

Inclusion is a central principle of Restorative Justice, emphasizing the importance of involving all stakeholders in the justice process. Unlike traditional justice systems, which typically marginalize victims and focus on state-imposed punishments, RJ actively includes the victim, offender, and community in the process of finding solutions. Inclusion fosters dialogue, understanding, and collaboration, ensuring that all voices are heard and respected.

In juvenile justice, inclusion is particularly important because young offenders are still in the process of developing their social and moral identities. The active involvement of victims, family members, and community representatives creates a supportive environment in which juveniles can learn from their mistakes and engage in constructive problem-solving.

- Victim Participation: RJ gives victims a platform to express their feelings, share their experiences, and communicate their needs. Victims are not passive observers but active participants in the process. This can provide a sense of closure and validation for victims, who often feel sidelined in traditional justice systems.

- Offender Engagement: Juveniles are not only held accountable for their actions but are also invited to participate in the creation of solutions. This helps offenders feel more connected to the outcome and more motivated to follow through on agreements made during the restorative process.

- Community Involvement: The community plays a critical role in RJ by providing support to both the victim and the offender. Community members may be involved in facilitating dialogue, offering resources for rehabilitation, or monitoring restitution agreements. This collective participation reinforces the idea that crime affects everyone and that solutions must be found collaboratively.

Inclusion ensures that the justice process is not limited to legal professionals but is instead a communal effort that promotes healing, learning, and social cohesion. For juvenile offenders, this inclusive approach fosters a deeper connection to their community and a stronger sense of belonging, which is essential for rehabilitation.

2.3.4 Reintegration

Reintegration focuses on helping the offender return to society as a responsible and contributing member. Restorative Justice is not merely concerned with punishment or reparation but with ensuring that the offender is successfully reintegrated into the community, reducing the likelihood of future criminal behavior. For juveniles, who are still in the process of developing their identities and social roles, reintegration is a crucial element of justice.

Punitive approaches to juvenile justice often isolate young offenders, stigmatizing them and making it difficult for them to return to their families, schools, or communities. This alienation can lead to higher rates of recidivism as juveniles struggle to find a place in society after serving their punishment. Restorative Justice, by contrast, prioritizes reintegration and offers pathways for offenders to repair their relationships with the community.

- Addressing Root Causes: Reintegration involves addressing the underlying causes of the offender's behavior, such as family dysfunction, poverty, trauma, or lack of educational opportunities. By addressing these root causes, RJ helps juveniles avoid the conditions that may lead to further offending.

- Support Networks: RJ provides juveniles with support networks that include family members, mentors, community leaders, and social services. These networks help guide juveniles through the process of reintegration and provide the resources they need to succeed.

- Reducing Stigma: Reintegration also involves reducing the stigma associated with criminal behavior. RJ encourages the community to see juvenile offenders not as lost causes but as individuals capable of growth and change. This shift in perception is vital for creating a supportive environment for rehabilitation.

Reintegration is essential for preventing recidivism and helping juvenile offenders find their place in society. By focusing on long-term solutions that address the root causes of criminal behavior and provide support, RJ promotes the successful reintegration of juvenile offenders, ultimately contributing to safer and more cohesive communities.

In summary, the key principles of Restorative Justice — accountability, reparation, inclusion, and reintegration — form the foundation of an approach to justice that emphasizes healing, responsibility, and social restoration. For juvenile offenders, these principles offer a pathway to personal growth, rehabilitation, and successful reintegration into society. Through active participation in the justice process, juvenile offenders can learn from their mistakes, make amends, and develop the skills and understanding necessary to avoid future offending. Restorative Justice offers a humane and effective alternative to punitive approaches, creating opportunities for both offenders and communities to heal and move forward.

2.4 Theoretical Foundations of Restorative Justice

Restorative Justice (RJ) is supported by various theoretical frameworks that provide a foundation for its principles and practices. These frameworks help to explain why RJ is an effective and necessary alternative to punitive justice systems, particularly in addressing juvenile crime. Theories such as Social Constructivism, Conflict Resolution

Theory, and Communitarian Theory offer insights into how crime is understood, how harm can be repaired, and the role of the community in rehabilitation. These theories reinforce the idea that crime is not merely a violation of law but a disruption to relationships and social harmony that must be addressed through collaborative and inclusive processes.

2.4.1 Social Constructivism

Social Constructivism is a theoretical framework that views crime as a social construct rather than an inherent moral wrong. In this perspective, crime is understood as behavior that violates the social norms and expectations of a given community or society. The focus is not just on the legal breach but on the breakdown in relationships and social structures that crime causes. This theory emphasizes the importance of addressing the relational aspects of crime, particularly how it affects individuals and the community at large.

Restorative Justice, when viewed through the lens of Social Constructivism, focuses on repairing the relationships that have been damaged by the offender's actions. RJ does not see the offender as a "bad person" but rather as someone who has acted in a way that disrupts social harmony. The goal of RJ is to restore that harmony by facilitating communication between the offender, the victim, and the community, helping them to understand the impact of the offense and work toward reconciliation.

For juvenile offenders, Social Constructivism is particularly relevant because it emphasizes the role of social influences and relationships in shaping behavior. Juveniles are often more susceptible to external pressures, such as peer influence or challenging family environments, which can contribute to delinquency. RJ, grounded in this theory, helps to address these underlying social dynamics by involving the offender's family, community, and support systems in the restorative process.

Key aspects of Social Constructivism in RJ include:

- Crime as a Social Harm: Crime is seen as an act that harms relationships and social order, rather than simply a violation of legal rules.

- Restoration of Relationships: The primary aim of RJ is to repair the relationships between the offender, the victim, and the community.

- Collaborative Process: Restorative practices involve all stakeholders in finding solutions to address the harm caused, rather than imposing top-down punishment.

In the context of juvenile justice, Social Constructivism supports RJ's focus on the developmental and social needs of young offenders, helping them to repair relationships and reintegrate into society.

2.4.2 Conflict Resolution Theory

Conflict Resolution Theory is another critical theoretical foundation of Restorative Justice. This theory suggests that conflict, including criminal acts, can be resolved not through coercion or punishment, but through dialogue, cooperation, and problem-solving. Conflict Resolution Theory posits that crimes create conflicts between individuals (offender and victim), as well as between the offender and the community, which can only be effectively addressed through communication and mutual understanding.

In the traditional punitive justice system, the focus is on punishing the offender, often leading to further alienation and unresolved conflict. RJ, however, aligns with Conflict Resolution Theory by promoting constructive dialogue between the offender, victim, and community. The goal is to resolve the conflict created by the offense in a way that addresses the needs of all parties, promotes healing, and prevents future harm.

For juveniles, this approach is particularly beneficial as it encourages them to engage in meaningful dialogue about their actions and the consequences of those actions. Conflict resolution within RJ processes allows juvenile offenders to understand the harm they have caused, listen to the victim's perspective, and work collaboratively to find solutions. This helps to foster accountability and emotional growth, reducing the likelihood of future conflicts or offenses.

Key principles of Conflict Resolution Theory in RJ include:

- Dialogue and Cooperation: Rather than relying on punitive measures, RJ emphasizes open communication and cooperative problem-solving to resolve the conflict created by the offense.

- Focus on Relationships: Conflict is seen as a disruption in relationships that can be repaired through understanding, empathy, and negotiation.

- Voluntary Participation: In RJ processes, all parties participate voluntarily, contributing to a more genuine resolution and a greater sense of ownership over the outcome.

In the juvenile justice context, Conflict Resolution Theory helps to create an environment where young offenders can learn from their mistakes, develop empathy for others, and actively participate in resolving the harm caused by their actions.

2.4.3 Communitarian Theory

Communitarian Theory suggests that individuals are not isolated beings but are deeply influenced by the communities to which they belong. According to this theory, individuals' behavior is shaped by their relationships, social networks, and the norms of their communities. Crime, from a communitarian perspective, is a breakdown in the social fabric of the community, and it is the community's responsibility to help address and repair this breakdown.

Restorative Justice aligns closely with Communitarian Theory by emphasizing the role of the community in both the offense and the healing process. RJ processes are designed to involve the community in addressing crime, helping to reintegrate the offender, and providing support for the victim. The belief is that the community plays a crucial role in preventing crime, supporting rehabilitation, and maintaining social order. This stands in contrast to traditional justice systems, which often isolate the offender from the community through incarceration or other punitive measures.

For juvenile offenders, the community plays an especially important role. Adolescents are still in the process of forming their identities, and their behavior is strongly influenced by their environment. Communitarian Theory suggests that community involvement in the justice process can help guide young offenders back onto a positive path. By involving community members, such as family, teachers, and mentors, RJ creates a supportive network that helps the juvenile offender to reintegrate, learn from their mistakes, and make amends.

Key aspects of Communitarian Theory in RJ include:

- Community Involvement: The community is seen as an essential actor in the justice process, playing a role in both supporting the victim and rehabilitating the offender.

- Social Responsibility: Crime is viewed as a community issue, and the community must take collective responsibility for addressing the harm and preventing future offenses.

- Reintegration: The community plays a key role in helping the offender reintegrate and avoid further criminal behavior, rather than isolating or stigmatizing the individual.

In juvenile justice, Communitarian Theory supports the idea that rehabilitation and reintegration are most effective when the community is actively involved in supporting the young offender's development and socialization.

Conclusion

Restorative Justice is grounded in several theoretical perspectives that emphasize relationships, dialogue, and community involvement in the justice process. Social Constructivism frames crime as a social harm that requires the repair of relationships, Conflict Resolution Theory advocates for dialogue and cooperation in resolving the conflict caused by crime, and Communitarian Theory highlights the role of the community in shaping behavior and promoting reintegration. These theoretical foundations provide a robust framework for understanding why RJ is particularly effective for juveniles, who are still developing socially and emotionally, and whose behavior is often influenced by their relationships and environment. By focusing on healing, accountability, and collaboration, RJ offers a more constructive and humane approach to juvenile justice, addressing both the needs of the offender and the broader community.

CHAPTER 03

JUVENILE JUSTICE SYSTEM

3.1 Traditional vs. Restorative Approaches

Juvenile justice systems have historically been modeled after adult criminal justice frameworks, where the focus is primarily on deterrence, punishment, and retribution. In traditional systems, the primary goal is to maintain law and order by imposing penalties on offenders to discourage future criminal behavior, both for the individual and society at large. Juveniles in these systems are often treated similarly to adults, despite significant differences in their cognitive, emotional, and social development. Over time, however, increasing evidence has shown that these punitive measures often fail to rehabilitate young offenders and may even exacerbate the problem. As a result, many countries have begun adopting Restorative Justice (RJ) as a more developmentally appropriate and effective alternative for addressing juvenile crime. RJ focuses on repairing harm, promoting accountability, and supporting the reintegration of young offenders into their communities.

Traditional Juvenile Justice Approach

In traditional juvenile justice systems, the response to juvenile crime is typically adversarial, punitive, and centered on the idea of deterrence. The legal process often mirrors adult criminal proceedings, with the following characteristics:

1. Punitive Focus: The central focus of traditional juvenile justice is on punishment. Juveniles are subject to a range of punitive sanctions, including detention, incarceration, probation, and fines. The severity of the punishment is often proportionate to the offense, with the goal of deterring future criminal behavior. This approach assumes that harsh penalties will discourage not only the individual offender but also other potential offenders from committing similar crimes.

2. Incarceration and Detention: One of the most common punitive measures in traditional systems is the use of detention or incarceration, where juveniles are placed in

juvenile detention centers or correctional facilities. These environments often isolate young offenders from their families, schools, and communities, and expose them to other delinquent peers, increasing the risk of recidivism. Research has shown that incarceration can be particularly harmful to juveniles, as it interrupts their education, social development, and psychological well-being.

3. Stigmatization and Labeling: Traditional justice systems can lead to the stigmatization and labeling of juvenile offenders. Once labeled as "delinquent" or "criminal," young offenders may struggle to reintegrate into society, facing difficulties in securing employment, continuing their education, or repairing relationships with their families and communities. This stigma can reinforce criminal identities, making it more difficult for juveniles to break the cycle of offending.

4. Focus on Guilt and Legal Processes: The traditional approach places a heavy emphasis on determining guilt and administering punishment. Juvenile offenders are often processed through formal court systems, with little attention paid to the underlying causes of their behavior, such as family dysfunction, trauma, poverty, or lack of educational support. The legal process can be intimidating and alienating for young offenders, who may not fully understand the consequences of their actions or the legal procedures they are subjected to.

5. Limited Victim Involvement: In traditional systems, victims of juvenile crime are often sidelined, with little opportunity to participate in the justice process or express their needs. The focus is primarily on punishing the offender, rather than addressing the harm done to the victim or repairing the damage to relationships and communities.

While the traditional juvenile justice system seeks to maintain order and discourage future crime, it often fails to address the root causes of juvenile offending. The reliance on punitive measures can lead to high recidivism rates, as young offenders are not provided with the tools or support needed to change their behavior. Additionally, the adversarial nature of the traditional system can further alienate juveniles from their communities, reinforcing patterns of delinquency.

Restorative Justice Approach to Juvenile Offending

In contrast, the Restorative Justice approach to juvenile offending focuses on healing, accountability, and reintegration, recognizing that juveniles are still developing and therefore more amenable to rehabilitation. RJ is designed to be developmentally appropriate, offering a more holistic and community-centered approach to addressing juvenile crime. Key distinctions between RJ and traditional approaches include the following:

1. Repairing Harm Over Punishment: In RJ, the primary goal is to repair the harm caused by the offense rather than to punish the offender. RJ recognizes that crime affects not only the victim but also the offender, the community, and the relationships among them. The focus is on addressing the needs of all parties involved—victims, offenders, and the community—through processes that promote dialogue, understanding, and mutual agreement on how to make amends.

2. Community and Family Involvement: RJ actively involves the community and the offender's family in the justice process. Practices such as Family Group Conferencing (FGC) and Restorative Circles bring together the offender, victim, family members, and community representatives to discuss the offense, its impact, and the steps needed to repair the harm. This collaborative process fosters a sense of collective responsibility and support, helping juveniles to feel connected to their community and providing them with the resources they need to avoid future offending.

3. Accountability and Personal Growth: RJ emphasizes the importance of accountability, not as a form of punishment, but as a means of fostering personal growth and responsibility. Juvenile offenders are encouraged to take responsibility for their actions by acknowledging the harm they have caused and actively participating in repairing it. This

process often involves direct dialogue with the victim, where the offender has the opportunity to apologize, listen to the victim's perspective, and make amends through restitution, community service, or other reparative actions. This emphasis on accountability helps juveniles develop empathy, self-reflection, and problem-solving skills, which are crucial for their rehabilitation and future development.

4. Victim-Centered Approach: Unlike traditional systems, which often marginalize victims, RJ places a strong emphasis on victim involvement. Victims are given a voice in the justice process and have the opportunity to express how the crime has affected them, their needs, and what they would like to see done to repair the harm. This victim-centered approach promotes healing and reconciliation, as victims are not only able to receive restitution but also to experience a sense of closure and empowerment through their active participation.

5. Reintegration and Rehabilitation: The ultimate goal of RJ is to reintegrate the offender into society as a responsible and contributing member, rather than isolating or stigmatizing them. RJ recognizes that many juvenile offenders come from challenging backgrounds and that their behavior is often influenced by external factors such as trauma, poverty, or family dysfunction. RJ processes are designed to

address these root causes by providing juveniles with support networks, educational opportunities, counseling, and mentorship, all aimed at promoting rehabilitation and preventing recidivism.

6. Focus on Developmental Needs: RJ recognizes that juveniles are in a unique stage of psychological and emotional development. Their cognitive abilities, decision-making processes, and understanding of consequences are still maturing, making them more responsive to interventions that emphasize learning and growth rather than punishment. RJ processes are tailored to the developmental needs of juveniles, providing them with the opportunity to reflect on their actions, understand the impact on others, and develop the skills necessary for successful reintegration into society.

7. Lower Recidivism Rates: Empirical evidence suggests that RJ is more effective than traditional punitive approaches in reducing recidivism among juvenile offenders. By focusing on rehabilitation, accountability, and community support, RJ helps juveniles develop a sense of responsibility and empathy, which are key factors in preventing reoffending. RJ also helps to break the cycle of criminal behavior by addressing the underlying issues that contribute to delinquency, such as family dysfunction, substance abuse, and lack of educational support.

Conclusion

The distinction between traditional and Restorative Justice approaches to juvenile crime highlights two fundamentally different philosophies of justice. Traditional systems, with their emphasis on punishment and deterrence, often fail to address the developmental needs of juveniles and can lead to negative outcomes such as stigmatization and high recidivism rates. In contrast, Restorative Justice offers a more constructive, inclusive, and rehabilitative approach, focusing on repairing harm, fostering accountability, and supporting the reintegration of young offenders into their communities. By recognizing that juveniles are still developing and are capable of change, RJ provides a more effective and humane response to juvenile crime, one that benefits not only the offender but also the victim and the broader community.

3.2 Models of Restorative Justice in Juvenile Systems

Restorative Justice (RJ) offers various models tailored to address juvenile offending by promoting healing, accountability, and reintegration. The following are key models utilized within juvenile justice systems:

Victim-Offender Mediation (VOM)

Definition:

Victim-Offender Mediation is a facilitated process where juvenile offenders meet their victims in a controlled and safe environment to discuss the offense, its impact, and agree on steps to repair the harm caused.

Key Features:

- Direct Dialogue: Allows for face-to-face communication between the victim and the offender.

- Facilitated by a Mediator: A neutral third party guides the conversation to ensure productive and respectful interaction.

- Voluntary Participation: Both parties choose to engage in the process willingly.

- Focus on Accountability: Encourages the offender to take responsibility for their actions.

- Development of a Restitution Plan: Collaborative agreement on how the offender can make amends.

Application in Juvenile Justice:

- Emotional Impact on Offenders: Facing their victims can help juveniles understand the real-life consequences of their actions.

- Empowerment of Victims: Provides victims a voice and an opportunity to express their feelings and needs.

- Reduction in Recidivism: Studies have shown that VOM can lead to lower reoffending rates among juveniles.

- Customization of Outcomes: Solutions are tailored to fit the specific circumstances of the offense and the needs of those involved.

Example:

In Germany, VOM has been integrated into the juvenile justice system, allowing young offenders to engage directly with victims, leading to meaningful restitution agreements and positive behavioral changes.

Family Group Conferencing (FGC)

Definition:

Family Group Conferencing involves the offender, the victim, their families, and sometimes community supporters in a meeting to collectively decide on an appropriate resolution to the offense.

Key Features:

- Inclusive Participation: Brings together all stakeholders affected by the juvenile's actions.

- Preparation Phase: Facilitators meet with participants individually beforehand to prepare them for the conference.

- Collaborative Decision-Making: The group works together to develop a plan that addresses the harm and outlines steps for reparation.

- Support Networks: Leverages family and community resources to support the offender's rehabilitation.

Application in Juvenile Justice:

- Cultural Sensitivity: Adaptable to various cultural contexts, respecting family structures and community norms.

- Strengthening Family Bonds: Engages the family in the juvenile's rehabilitation process, which can be crucial for long-term success.

- Victim Satisfaction: Victims often report higher satisfaction due to their active role in the resolution process.

- Holistic Approach: Addresses underlying issues contributing to the offender's behavior, such as family dynamics or social influences.

Example:

New Zealand's juvenile justice system widely uses FGC, rooted in Maori practices, resulting in decreased youth incarceration rates and improved outcomes for young offenders.

Restorative Circles

Definition:

Restorative Circles are community meetings where the offender, victim, and other affected parties sit in a circle to discuss the offense, its impact, and collectively agree on steps to repair the harm.

Key Features:

- Equal Footing: The circular seating arrangement symbolizes equality among participants.

- Facilitated Dialogue: A circle keeper guides the discussion, ensuring everyone has the opportunity to speak.

- Community Engagement: Involves peers, teachers, or community members who can support the offender's reintegration.

- Consensus-Based Outcomes: Decisions are made collaboratively, reflecting the shared values of the group.

Application in Juvenile Justice:

- Empathy Development: Encourages juveniles to understand and empathize with those affected by their actions.

- Community Support: Builds a network of support for the offender, aiding in rehabilitation.

- Conflict Resolution Skills: Teaches juveniles constructive ways to handle disputes.

- Preventative Potential: Can be used proactively in schools or communities to address issues before they escalate.

Example:

In Brazil, Restorative Circles have been implemented in schools to address minor offenses, resulting in improved school climates and reduced disciplinary incidents.

Community Restorative Boards

Definition:

Community Restorative Boards consist of trained community volunteers who meet with offenders and sometimes victims to develop restitution agreements and oversee the offender's progress.

Key Features:

- Community Representation: Board members reflect the community's values and norms.

- Restitution Planning: Collaboratively create a plan for the offender to make amends.

- Monitoring and Support: Boards track the offender's compliance and provide guidance.

- Educational Component: Focus on helping the offender understand the impact of their actions.

Application in Juvenile Justice:

- Accountability to the Community: Offenders recognize their responsibility not just to the victim but to the broader community.

- Skill Development: Programs may include workshops on life skills, decision-making, or employment readiness.

- Reintegration Focus: Supports juveniles in becoming productive community members.

- Diversion from Formal System: Offers an alternative to formal judicial proceedings, reducing the likelihood of incarceration.

Example:

In Vermont, USA, Community Justice Centers utilize restorative panels for juveniles, resulting in high completion rates of restitution agreements and positive feedback from participants.

Overall Impact on Juvenile Justice Systems:

- Reduced Recidivism: Restorative models have been associated with lower reoffending rates among juveniles.

- Victim Satisfaction: Active involvement and restitution contribute to higher satisfaction levels for victims.

- Cost-Effectiveness: These approaches can be more cost-effective than traditional incarceration.

- Positive Behavioral Changes: Offenders often exhibit improved behavior and decision-making skills post-participation.

- Community Cohesion: Strengthens community ties by involving members in the justice process and emphasizing collective responsibility.

By integrating these restorative models, juvenile justice systems can more effectively address the unique needs of young offenders, promote healing for victims, and enhance community well-being.

3.3 Implementation of Restorative Justice in Different Jurisdictions

The implementation of Restorative Justice (RJ) in juvenile justice systems has gained momentum globally, with countries such as New Zealand, Canada, and the United States leading the way. These countries have integrated RJ practices into their juvenile justice systems, offering alternatives to punitive measures like incarceration and instead focusing on rehabilitation, reconciliation, and community involvement. The following section explores how RJ has been applied in different jurisdictions, highlighting key models and their impact on juvenile offenders, victims, and communities.

New Zealand: Family Group Conferencing (FGC)

New Zealand is often recognized as a global leader in the integration of Restorative Justice into its juvenile justice system. The cornerstone of this approach is the Family Group Conferencing (FGC) model, which has been in place since the enactment of the Children, Young Persons, and Their Families Act 1989.

Key Features of FGC in New Zealand:

- Legally Mandated for Juveniles: FGC is a mandatory process for juveniles who commit offenses, ensuring that restorative practices are at the heart of New Zealand's juvenile justice system.

- Holistic Approach: The process involves the juvenile offender, the victim, their families, and other community members to discuss the offense, its impact, and how the harm can be repaired.

- Collaborative Decision-Making: All parties work together to create a restorative plan that outlines steps for the offender to make amends. This could involve restitution, community service, or therapy.

- Emphasis on Reconciliation: FGC promotes reconciliation by allowing victims to have their voices heard and empowering offenders to take responsibility for their actions.

Impact in New Zealand:

- Reduction in Juvenile Incarceration Rates: Since the introduction of FGC, New Zealand has seen a significant decline in the number of juveniles incarcerated. The focus on resolving the root causes of offending behavior through family and community support has contributed to lower recidivism rates.

- High Satisfaction Rates: Both victims and offenders report high levels of satisfaction with the FGC process, as it provides a space for healing, accountability, and personal growth.

- Cultural Sensitivity: FGC is heavily influenced by Maori traditions, reflecting New Zealand's commitment to integrating indigenous perspectives on justice. This cultural sensitivity has made the RJ process more inclusive and effective in addressing the needs of Maori youth, who are overrepresented in the criminal justice system.

Canada: Victim-Offender Mediation and Sentencing Circles

Canada has also been a pioneer in the implementation of RJ in juvenile justice, with models like Victim-Offender Mediation (VOM) and Sentencing Circles being widely adopted.

Victim-Offender Mediation (VOM) in Canada:

- Direct Dialogue: VOM provides an opportunity for juvenile offenders to meet with their victims in a safe, mediated environment to discuss the offense and agree on how to repair the harm.

- Voluntary Participation: Both parties must agree to participate in the process, which ensures that the mediation is driven by mutual consent and willingness to resolve the conflict.

- Restitution Agreements: The outcome of VOM typically involves a restitution plan that could include financial compensation, community service, or a formal apology.

Sentencing Circles:

- Community Involvement: Sentencing Circles, inspired by indigenous practices, involve the offender, victim, and community members in a circle discussion to decide on a restorative response to the offense.

- Collaborative Justice: The circle process allows for community input into the sentencing decision, emphasizing healing for all parties rather than punishment alone.

- Incorporation of Indigenous Practices: Sentencing Circles reflect the values of indigenous communities in Canada, where justice is seen as a communal responsibility. These practices have been particularly effective in reducing recidivism among indigenous youth, who are disproportionately represented in the justice system.

Impact in Canada:

- Reduction in Recidivism: Studies have shown that juveniles who participate in VOM and Sentencing Circles are less likely to reoffend, as the restorative process helps them understand the impact of their actions and encourages personal accountability.

- Empowerment of Victims: Victims who engage in these restorative processes report higher levels of satisfaction and a sense of closure, as they are given the opportunity to directly communicate with the offender and participate in shaping the resolution.

- Focus on Rehabilitation: By involving the community and addressing the underlying causes of criminal behavior, Canada's RJ programs for juveniles emphasize rehabilitation over punishment, fostering long-term behavioral change.

United States: Diversion Programs and Community Restorative Boards

In the United States, several states have incorporated Restorative Justice practices into their juvenile justice systems, with a focus on diversion programs and Community Restorative Boards.

Diversion Programs in the U.S.:

- Pre-Court Intervention: Many states offer RJ programs as diversion options, meaning that juveniles can participate in restorative processes like mediation, family conferencing, or community service in lieu of formal court proceedings.

- Rehabilitation Focus: Diversion programs aim to prevent juveniles from entering the formal justice system, recognizing that early intervention and community-based solutions are more effective in preventing future offending.

Community Restorative Boards:

- Community-Led Restorative Justice: In several states, Community Restorative Boards are composed of trained community volunteers who meet with the juvenile offender and sometimes the victim to develop a restitution plan.

- Monitoring and Support: The boards also monitor the juvenile's progress in fulfilling the restitution agreement, providing guidance and support to ensure successful completion.

Examples of U.S. RJ Initiatives:

- Vermont: Vermont has been a leader in RJ, with community-based justice programs that use restorative panels to resolve juvenile offenses. These panels work with juveniles to create tailored restitution agreements and offer support for reintegration.

- Minnesota: Minnesota has implemented RJ programs in schools and juvenile courts, using mediation and conferencing to resolve conflicts and prevent escalation into more serious criminal behavior.

Impact in the United States:

- Reduced Court Caseloads: Diversion programs have significantly reduced the number of juveniles entering the formal justice system, relieving pressure on courts and correctional facilities.

- Lower Recidivism Rates: Juveniles who participate in RJ programs in the U.S. have shown lower recidivism rates compared to those processed through traditional juvenile courts.

- Restorative Culture in Schools: RJ practices in schools, such as restorative circles, have helped to reduce disciplinary issues and promote a culture of conflict resolution, reducing the likelihood that juvenile conflicts escalate into criminal behavior.

Comparison and Key Insights

Across these jurisdictions, the implementation of Restorative Justice in juvenile systems has proven to be effective in reducing recidivism, promoting victim satisfaction, and fostering the rehabilitation of young offenders. Some common insights include:

- Tailored Solutions: RJ processes are adaptable to different cultural contexts, with New Zealand's FGC model reflecting Maori values and Canada's Sentencing Circles honoring indigenous traditions.

- Victim Empowerment: In all three jurisdictions, RJ provides victims with a platform to express their needs and contribute to the resolution, leading to higher satisfaction and emotional healing.

- Focus on Rehabilitation: By emphasizing accountability, restitution, and reintegration, RJ helps juvenile offenders make amends and avoid future criminal behavior.

Each of these jurisdictions highlights the potential of RJ to transform juvenile justice systems by focusing on healing, community involvement, and positive outcomes for all parties involved. Through its implementation, RJ has demonstrated that rehabilitation and accountability can coexist, offering a more effective and humane response to juvenile crime.

3.4 Case Studies

Restorative Justice (RJ) has been implemented in various jurisdictions, with significant success in reducing recidivism among juveniles, promoting rehabilitation, and enhancing victim satisfaction. In addition to the widely recognized Family Group Conferencing model in New Zealand and the Restorative Justice initiatives in Minnesota, other case studies provide further evidence of RJ's effectiveness in juvenile justice systems. This section explores additional case studies from Canada, Belgium, and South

Africa, illustrating the diverse applications and positive outcomes of RJ in juvenile contexts.

New Zealand's Family Group Conferencing (FGC) Model

Overview:

In New Zealand, the Family Group Conferencing (FGC) model has been institutionalized nationwide since the passage of the Children, Young Persons, and Their Families Act 1989. The model brings together juvenile offenders, their victims, family members, and other community stakeholders to collaboratively negotiate a resolution to the offense. The conference aims to repair the harm caused, hold the juvenile accountable, and develop a restitution plan that promotes rehabilitation.

Impact:

- Reduction in Recidivism: New Zealand has reported significant declines in recidivism among juveniles who participate in FGCs. The model's focus on family involvement, community support, and victim participation creates a comprehensive approach to rehabilitation that addresses the underlying causes of juvenile offending.

- Cultural Relevance: The model is grounded in Maori traditions, which emphasize collective responsibility and reconciliation, making it particularly effective in addressing the needs of indigenous youth, who are overrepresented in the criminal justice system.

- Victim Satisfaction: Victims often report high levels of satisfaction with the FGC process, as it provides them with an opportunity to voice their concerns, receive apologies, and participate in shaping the outcome.

Minnesota's Restorative Justice Initiatives

Overview:

Minnesota has been a leader in integrating RJ into its juvenile justice system. The state has implemented various RJ programs, including victim-offender mediation, community service programs, and restorative circles, which aim to address juvenile offenses outside the traditional court system.

Impact:

- Reduced Recidivism: Empirical data suggest that juveniles who participate in RJ programs in Minnesota are significantly less likely to reoffend compared to those who go through the traditional juvenile justice process.

- Victim Empowerment: RJ initiatives in Minnesota emphasize the importance of victim involvement, giving victims a platform to share their experiences and engage directly with offenders. This has resulted in greater victim satisfaction and a sense of closure.

- Community Involvement: Minnesota's RJ programs engage community volunteers, who work with offenders to develop restitution plans and monitor progress, promoting community accountability and support for juvenile rehabilitation.

Canada: Victim-Offender Mediation and Sentencing Circles

Overview:

Canada has integrated Restorative Justice practices into its juvenile justice system through programs such as Victim-Offender Mediation (VOM) and Sentencing Circles, both of which have proven effective in reducing recidivism among indigenous and non-indigenous youth.

Impact:

- Successful Reintegration: Sentencing Circles, modeled after First Nations traditions, involve community members, victims, and offenders in dialogue to find a restorative solution to the crime. This process emphasizes the importance of community support in the reintegration of young offenders.

- Recidivism Reduction: Juveniles who participate in these RJ processes are less likely to reoffend. The focus on repairing relationships and involving the offender in the development of restitution plans contributes to long-term behavior change.

- Cultural Sensitivity: The inclusion of indigenous practices in the justice process addresses the unique needs of indigenous youth, providing culturally relevant solutions that strengthen their connection to their communities and reduce the likelihood of reoffending.

Belgium: Restorative Justice in Juvenile Institutions

Overview:

Belgium has incorporated RJ into its juvenile justice system, particularly within juvenile detention centers. Through the use of restorative dialogues and mediation, Belgium has successfully integrated RJ practices into institutional settings.

Impact:

- Restorative Mediation in Institutions: Juveniles in detention participate in mediation sessions with their victims, often resulting in formal apologies, restitution agreements, and conflict resolution. This model allows juveniles to take responsibility for their actions even within the confines of a detention center, promoting rehabilitation and emotional development.

- Post-Release Support: Belgium's RJ programs extend beyond the institutional setting, offering ongoing support to juveniles upon release to ensure they are reintegrated into society successfully. This holistic approach has contributed to lower recidivism rates and smoother transitions for juveniles returning to their communities.

South Africa: Diversion Programs for Juveniles

Overview:

In South Africa, RJ plays a crucial role in juvenile diversion programs, which aim to keep young offenders out of the formal criminal justice system. These programs focus on dialogue, restitution, and community service, offering alternatives to traditional punitive measures.

Impact:

- High Success Rate in Diversion: South Africa's RJ diversion programs have demonstrated a high success rate in preventing juveniles from entering the formal justice system. By addressing offenses through RJ practices such as mediation and conferencing, these programs reduce the likelihood of incarceration and reoffending.

- Youth Empowerment: Juveniles who participate in diversion programs are often required to complete community service or engage in other reparative actions, helping them to develop a sense of responsibility and civic engagement.

- Community Healing: The involvement of community leaders and families in RJ processes has helped to strengthen social bonds and promote collective healing in communities affected by crime.

Norway: Restorative Circles in Schools

Overview:

Norway has implemented Restorative Circles in schools as part of its broader effort to address juvenile conflict and crime before it escalates to more serious offenses. These circles provide a safe space for juveniles, teachers, victims, and community members to discuss the offense and agree on a path toward resolution.

Impact:

- Prevention of Juvenile Crime: Restorative Circles in schools have been successful in preventing conflicts from escalating into criminal behavior. By addressing issues early, these programs help juveniles develop conflict resolution skills and avoid more serious offenses.

- Reduction in School-Based Violence: The implementation of RJ in schools has contributed to a decrease in violence and bullying, as students learn to communicate and resolve conflicts constructively.

- Long-Term Behavioral Change: By teaching juveniles the value of dialogue and empathy, Norway's RJ programs in schools have helped to promote long-term behavioral change, reducing the likelihood of future offenses.

Conclusion

These case studies demonstrate the wide-ranging success of Restorative Justice in juvenile systems across the globe. From New Zealand's Family Group Conferencing model to South Africa's diversion programs and Belgium's use of RJ in juvenile institutions, the evidence shows that RJ not only reduces recidivism but also promotes victim satisfaction, rehabilitation, and community healing. By focusing on accountability, dialogue, and reintegration, RJ offers a more effective and humane alternative to traditional punitive approaches in juvenile justice.

CHAPTER 04

THE IMPACT OF RESTORATIVE JUSTICE ON RECIDIVISIM AMD REHABILITATION

4.1 Reducing Recidivism

Reducing recidivism, or the likelihood of reoffending, is a central objective of juvenile justice systems around the world. Restorative Justice (RJ) has proven to be highly effective in achieving this goal by addressing the root causes of juvenile delinquency and creating pathways for rehabilitation and reintegration. Unlike traditional punitive justice systems, which often isolate and stigmatize offenders, RJ offers a holistic approach that emphasizes accountability, personal growth, and community involvement. Through RJ, juveniles have the opportunity to understand the impact of their actions, make amends, and rebuild their relationships with their families, victims, and communities. Studies conducted in various countries provide compelling evidence that RJ programs significantly reduce recidivism rates among juveniles compared to traditional punitive methods.

How Restorative Justice Reduces Recidivism

RJ reduces recidivism by focusing on several key factors:

- Addressing Underlying Causes of Crime: RJ emphasizes understanding the personal, social, and economic factors that contribute to juvenile offending, such as family dysfunction, peer pressure, substance abuse, trauma, and poverty. By addressing these root causes through tailored interventions—such as counseling, family support, educational programs, and community involvement—RJ helps prevent future criminal behavior.

- Promoting Accountability and Empathy: RJ encourages juvenile offenders to take responsibility for their actions and develop empathy for their victims. This direct engagement with the consequences of their behavior fosters emotional growth and moral development, reducing the likelihood of reoffending. Offenders learn to recognize the harm caused by their actions, thereby promoting behavioral change.

- Supporting Rehabilitation and Reintegration: By involving the community and the offender's family in the justice process, RJ creates a support network that helps juveniles reintegrate into society. This focus on reintegration reduces the risk of recidivism, as offenders are provided with guidance, mentorship, and opportunities to rebuild their lives in positive ways.

- Building Social and Emotional Skills: RJ programs teach juveniles essential skills such as conflict resolution, problem-solving, and emotional regulation, which are critical for avoiding future criminal behavior. These programs provide juveniles with tools to handle challenges in constructive ways rather than resorting to delinquency.

Global Studies on Restorative Justice and Recidivism Reduction

Several studies from different parts of the world demonstrate the effectiveness of RJ in reducing recidivism among juveniles.

New Zealand

Study Overview:

New Zealand's Family Group Conferencing (FGC) model has been at the forefront of RJ in the juvenile justice system. A 2016 government report analyzed recidivism rates among juveniles who participated in FGC compared to those processed through the traditional court system.

Findings:

- Juveniles who participated in FGC were less likely to reoffend than those who went through the traditional justice system.

- The success of FGC in reducing recidivism was attributed to its emphasis on family involvement and community support, which helped address the underlying social and emotional issues that led to offending.

- Victims who participated in FGC also reported a higher level of satisfaction, as they were able to engage directly with the offender, promoting healing and reducing the desire for punitive justice.

Conclusion:

New Zealand's FGC model has significantly contributed to lower recidivism rates, demonstrating that RJ processes can offer more sustainable outcomes than punitive measures.

United States: Minnesota's RJ Programs

Study Overview:

Minnesota has been a leader in implementing RJ programs for juveniles, particularly through victim-offender mediation, community panels, and diversion programs. A 2002 study by the Minnesota Department of Corrections examined the recidivism rates of juveniles who participated in RJ programs compared to those who went through traditional juvenile courts.

Findings:

- Juveniles who participated in RJ programs in Minnesota showed a 50% reduction in recidivism compared to those who were processed through the traditional juvenile court system.

- RJ participants were more likely to successfully complete restitution agreements and reintegrate into their communities without reoffending.

- The study also found that victim satisfaction rates were significantly higher in RJ programs, which contributed to greater emotional healing and community restoration.

Conclusion:

Minnesota's RJ programs have been instrumental in reducing juvenile recidivism by focusing on rehabilitation, community involvement, and restitution, rather than punishment.

Canada: Indigenous Sentencing Circles

Study Overview:

In Canada, the use of Sentencing Circles, particularly for indigenous juveniles, has been a key component of RJ practices. A study conducted by the Canadian Department of

Justice in 2015 examined the impact of Sentencing Circles on recidivism among indigenous youth, who are disproportionately represented in the juvenile justice system.

Findings:

- Indigenous juveniles who participated in Sentencing Circles had lower recidivism rates compared to those who went through the traditional juvenile justice system.

- The Sentencing Circles were particularly effective in addressing the cultural and social needs of indigenous youth, emphasizing community healing and reconnection with cultural identity as part of the restorative process.

- Community involvement in the Sentencing Circles helped reduce feelings of alienation among indigenous youth, promoting long-term behavioral change.

Conclusion:

Canada's Sentencing Circles have successfully reduced recidivism among indigenous juveniles by promoting culturally relevant, community-based solutions to juvenile offending.

United Kingdom: RJ in Schools

Study Overview:

A 2014 study conducted in the United Kingdom focused on the use of RJ practices, such as Restorative Circles, in schools to address juvenile offenses and conflicts. The study aimed to measure the impact of school-based RJ programs on the behavior of young offenders and their recidivism rates.

Findings:

- Schools that implemented RJ programs reported a significant reduction in school-based violence and conflicts.

- Juveniles who participated in RJ processes, such as mediation and restorative circles, were less likely to engage in further delinquent behavior both in and out of school.

- RJ helped students develop conflict resolution skills and increased their understanding of the consequences of their actions, leading to better behavioral outcomes and reduced recidivism.

Conclusion:

RJ programs in UK schools have proven effective in reducing juvenile crime and delinquency by addressing conflicts at an early stage and promoting positive behavioral change.

South Africa: Diversion Programs

Study Overview:

South Africa has implemented RJ-based diversion programs aimed at preventing juvenile offenders from entering the formal criminal justice system. A 2011 study by the Institute for Security Studies evaluated the effectiveness of these programs in reducing recidivism among juvenile offenders.

Findings:

- Juveniles who participated in RJ diversion programs were significantly less likely to reoffend compared to those who went through the traditional court system.

- The programs focused on rehabilitation, community service, and victim-offender mediation, providing juveniles with the opportunity to repair the harm caused and reintegrate into society.

- Juveniles reported feeling more supported by their communities after participating in RJ processes, which contributed to their reduced likelihood of reoffending.

Conclusion:

South Africa's RJ-based diversion programs have been effective in reducing recidivism by emphasizing restorative practices that promote healing, accountability, and reintegration.

Conclusion

The global body of evidence shows that Restorative Justice is highly effective in reducing recidivism among juvenile offenders. By addressing the underlying causes of crime, promoting personal accountability, and involving families, victims, and communities in the justice process, RJ provides a more constructive and rehabilitative alternative to traditional punitive approaches. The studies from New Zealand, the United States, Canada, the United Kingdom, and South Africa demonstrate that RJ programs lead to lower reoffending rates, greater victim satisfaction, and stronger community ties. As a result, RJ offers a sustainable model for reducing juvenile crime and fostering long-term rehabilitation and social reintegration.

4.2 Fostering Rehabilitation

Restorative Justice (RJ) is particularly effective in fostering rehabilitation among juvenile offenders by focusing on empathy, accountability, personal growth, and community reintegration. Unlike punitive justice systems, which emphasize punishment, RJ seeks to create an environment where juveniles can learn from their mistakes, develop a deeper understanding of the harm they have caused, and work actively to repair the damage. This process of reflection and restitution promotes the emotional, psychological, and social development necessary for true rehabilitation, reducing the likelihood of future offending.

Promoting Empathy and Accountability

One of the key elements of RJ in fostering rehabilitation is its ability to promote empathy and accountability. In many cases, juveniles engage in criminal behavior without fully understanding the impact of their actions on others. RJ processes, such as Victim-Offender Mediation (VOM) and Restorative Circles, provide juveniles with the opportunity to engage directly with the people they have harmed. This direct dialogue allows young offenders to hear firsthand how their actions have affected victims, fostering a deeper sense of empathy and personal responsibility.

- Empathy Development: By hearing the victim's perspective, juveniles are encouraged to put themselves in the victim's shoes, which can lead to a greater emotional understanding of the consequences of their behavior. This empathy is a crucial step in changing the mindset that may have contributed to the offense.

- Accountability: RJ emphasizes the importance of offenders taking responsibility for their actions. Juveniles are not passive recipients of punishment but active participants in the justice process, where they must acknowledge the harm they have caused and work toward making amends. This sense of ownership over their actions is essential for rehabilitation.

Example:

In Canada's RJ programs, the use of Victim-Offender Mediation has been particularly effective in fostering empathy among juvenile offenders. After engaging in dialogue with their victims, young offenders often express remorse and a commitment to changing their behavior. This direct engagement with the victim is often a transformative experience that leads to long-term behavioral change.

Encouraging Personal Growth and Self-Reflection

Restorative Justice provides juveniles with the opportunity to engage in self-reflection, which is a critical component of personal growth. RJ encourages young offenders to reflect on the reasons behind their behavior, whether it be peer pressure, family problems, or other external factors, and to consider how they can make different choices in the future. This reflective process helps juveniles understand their own motivations and learn how to manage the influences that may lead to criminal behavior.

- Personal Growth: RJ processes create a supportive environment where juveniles are encouraged to learn from their mistakes rather than being defined by them. Offenders are often required to engage in community service, educational programs, or therapy as part of their restitution plan, all of which contribute to personal development.

- Skill Building: Through RJ programs, juveniles develop essential life skills, such as conflict resolution, emotional regulation, and decision-making. These skills are crucial for avoiding future offending and for becoming productive members of society.

Example:

In the United States, Minnesota's RJ programs have incorporated community service and educational opportunities into their restitution plans. Juveniles who participate in these programs not only make amends for their actions but also gain valuable skills and experiences that help them reintegrate into their communities as responsible citizens.

Supporting Reintegration into Society

A key aspect of rehabilitation in Restorative Justice is the focus on reintegration. RJ processes are designed to prevent juveniles from being alienated or stigmatized by their communities, which is a common consequence of punitive justice systems. Instead, RJ emphasizes the importance of helping juveniles rebuild their relationships with family, peers, and the broader community. This community-centered approach is critical for long-term rehabilitation, as it provides juveniles with a support network that can guide them as they move forward in their lives.

- Community Involvement: RJ actively involves the community in the rehabilitation process, whether through Family Group Conferencing (FGC) or Community Restorative Boards. By engaging family members, community leaders, and peers, RJ helps create a network of support that encourages positive behavior and reduces the likelihood of reoffending.

- Restitution and Reconnection: Juveniles often participate in restitution activities, such as community service, that help them make amends for their actions while simultaneously reconnecting with their communities. This process of making amends fosters a sense of belonging and purpose, which is critical for preventing recidivism.

Example:

In New Zealand's Family Group Conferencing model, the emphasis on family and community involvement has proven to be highly effective in supporting the reintegration of young offenders. By involving families in the justice process, FGC strengthens family bonds and ensures that juveniles receive the emotional and social support necessary for their rehabilitation.

Addressing Underlying Causes of Offending

Restorative Justice programs are designed to address the underlying causes of juvenile offending, such as trauma, substance abuse, mental health issues, and family problems. By tackling these root causes, RJ programs provide juveniles with the tools and resources they need to change their behavior and avoid future involvement with the justice system.

- Tailored Interventions: RJ processes often include personalized intervention plans that are tailored to the specific needs of the juvenile. These plans may involve counseling, therapy, substance abuse treatment, or mentoring programs designed to address the factors contributing to the juvenile's behavior.

- Long-Term Support: RJ programs do not end once restitution is completed. Many programs provide ongoing support to ensure that juveniles continue to receive the guidance and resources they need to maintain positive changes.

Example:

In South Africa, RJ-based diversion programs focus on providing juveniles with access to counseling and support services that address the underlying causes of their behavior. These programs have been successful in reducing recidivism by offering long-term solutions to the challenges that contribute to juvenile crime, such as poverty, substance abuse, and family dysfunction.

Restorative Justice and Juvenile Rehabilitation: Global Perspectives

Across the globe, Restorative Justice has been shown to promote rehabilitation and reintegration in juvenile offenders, leading to more positive long-term outcomes compared to traditional punitive approaches. Here are a few examples:

- United Kingdom: School-based RJ programs have been particularly effective in fostering rehabilitation by addressing conflicts early and providing juveniles with the tools to manage disputes constructively. The use of Restorative Circles in schools has led to reductions in school-based violence and delinquency, helping students develop conflict resolution skills and avoid future criminal behavior.

- Belgium: In Belgium, the integration of RJ practices within juvenile detention centers has demonstrated success in promoting rehabilitation. By engaging in Restorative Mediation with their victims, juveniles in detention are given the opportunity to reflect on their actions and work towards personal growth and change, even while in custody.

Conclusion

Restorative Justice provides juveniles with a unique opportunity for rehabilitation by focusing on empathy, accountability, personal growth, and reintegration. Through RJ processes, young offenders are encouraged to take responsibility for their actions, make amends, and engage in meaningful self-reflection. By addressing the underlying causes of juvenile offending and involving the community in the rehabilitation process, RJ fosters long-term behavioral change and reduces the likelihood of reoffending. Globally, RJ programs have proven effective in helping juveniles reintegrate into society as law-abiding citizens, making RJ a valuable tool for juvenile justice systems seeking to promote rehabilitation over punishment.

4.3 Role of Community and Victim Participation

The effectiveness of Restorative Justice (RJ) programs in the juvenile justice system heavily relies on the active participation of both the community and the victims. RJ operates on the premise that crime not only harms individuals but also disrupts the relationships within the community. Therefore, it involves all stakeholders, including victims, offenders, and the broader community, in the justice process. This participatory approach ensures that the juvenile offender is not only held accountable but also supported in their rehabilitation and reintegration into society. For victims, RJ provides an opportunity to actively engage in the justice process, voice their concerns, and receive reparations, contributing to their emotional healing.

Community Participation in Restorative Justice

Community Involvement in RJ is essential because it recognizes that crime impacts the entire community, not just the victim and offender. Community members play a vital role in the healing process and help to reintegrate the juvenile offender. Community participation in RJ models, such as Restorative Circles or Community Restorative Boards, helps create a supportive environment where the offender can be held accountable while also being guided back to a constructive path.

Advantages of Community Participation:

1. Promotes Accountability: The community serves as an accountability mechanism for the juvenile offender. The presence of community members ensures that the offender understands the broader social impact of their actions, encouraging them to take responsibility.

2. Support for Reintegration: Community participation fosters a supportive environment for the juvenile's reintegration. The community often plays an active role in monitoring restitution agreements and providing mentorship or resources, which can be crucial for the successful rehabilitation of the juvenile.

3. Strengthens Social Bonds: Community involvement in the justice process helps rebuild trust and strengthens the bonds between individuals, which may have been damaged by

the offense. This collective effort to resolve conflict contributes to the social cohesion of the community.

4. Prevention of Future Crimes: A community that is engaged in the justice process is more likely to play a proactive role in preventing future offenses. By being actively involved in the rehabilitation of juvenile offenders, communities can address underlying social issues such as poverty, peer pressure, and family dysfunction that contribute to criminal behavior.

Disadvantages of Community Participation:

1. Risk of Stigmatization: While community involvement can support reintegration, it also carries the risk of stigmatizing the offender. If the community perceives the offender as a continual threat, they may isolate or label them, which can hinder their ability to rehabilitate.

2. Inconsistent Commitment: Community participation is only effective if members are genuinely committed to the RJ process. In some cases, there may be low engagement or a lack of willingness to participate, especially in larger or more transient communities. This can undermine the success of the RJ process.

3. Imbalance of Power: In some communities, power dynamics can impact the fairness of the RJ process. If certain community members dominate the conversation or impose

their views, the process may not be truly restorative, and the juvenile offender may feel marginalized or unfairly treated.

Victim Participation in Restorative Justice

Victim participation is another cornerstone of RJ, offering victims a chance to actively engage in the justice process. Unlike traditional justice systems, where victims often feel sidelined, RJ centers their role by providing them with a voice and the opportunity to confront the offender directly. Victims are involved in deciding how the harm should be repaired and are an integral part of the resolution.

Advantages of Victim Participation:

1. Emotional Healing and Closure: Victims often report higher levels of satisfaction with RJ because it allows them to express their feelings, explain the impact of the offense, and receive reparations. This personal involvement can lead to emotional healing and a greater sense of closure, which is often lacking in punitive justice systems.

2. Restitution and Reparation: Victims are directly involved in creating restitution plans, ensuring that the offender takes meaningful steps to make amends for the harm caused. This participatory role gives victims a sense of justice and control over the outcome, which may not be possible in traditional court proceedings.

3. Reduction of Fear and Tension: Meeting the offender face-to-face in a controlled, safe environment often helps victims to overcome fear or anxiety related to the offense. This confrontation can reduce negative emotions like anger, fear, or frustration and facilitate reconciliation.

4. Empowerment: In RJ, victims are empowered to be active agents in the justice process rather than passive observers. This active participation can help victims regain a sense of power and agency, especially after experiencing trauma or victimization.

Disadvantages of Victim Participation:

1. Emotional Burden: While participation in RJ can promote healing, it can also be emotionally taxing for some victims, particularly if they are not ready to face the offender. The emotional toll of revisiting the crime may outweigh the potential benefits, especially for victims of violent or traumatic offenses.

2. Risk of Retraumatization: Victims may feel retraumatized by confronting the offender, especially if the offender shows a lack of remorse or if the victim does not receive the level of restitution or closure they were expecting.

3. Imbalance of Power: Just as with community participation, power dynamics can influence the RJ process. In some cases, victims may feel pressured to forgive or reconcile when they are not emotionally prepared to do so. If

the process feels forced, it may not lead to genuine healing or resolution.

Future Impact of Community and Victim Participation

The involvement of the community and victims in RJ has the potential for far-reaching future impacts, particularly in the juvenile justice system. As RJ becomes more widely adopted, several long-term outcomes are likely to emerge:

1. Stronger Communities and Social Cohesion:

- As communities become more involved in the RJ process, there is an opportunity to strengthen social bonds and foster a culture of collective responsibility. Communities that actively participate in RJ are better equipped to prevent future crime by addressing underlying social issues, such as poverty, substance abuse, and family instability.

- By reinforcing social cohesion and trust, RJ creates a more resilient community where conflicts are more likely to be resolved peacefully and collaboratively.

2. Cultural Shift Toward Restorative Practices:

- With increasing participation in RJ, society may experience a broader cultural shift away from retributive justice toward restorative practices. This shift could lead to a more compassionate justice system where the focus is on healing, reintegration, and conflict resolution rather than punishment.

- Juveniles, in particular, benefit from this shift, as RJ offers a more developmentally appropriate response to juvenile crime, emphasizing rehabilitation and growth rather than punishment.

3. Empowerment of Victims:

- Victim participation in RJ is likely to lead to a future justice system where victim empowerment is prioritized. By centering the victim's role in the justice process, RJ can improve the emotional well-being of victims and ensure that justice outcomes are more responsive to their needs.

- This empowerment can also have a ripple effect, encouraging victims to remain engaged in their communities and even serve as advocates for RJ in the future.

4. Sustained Reduction in Recidivism:

- With the active involvement of the community and victims, RJ has the potential to create a sustained reduction in recidivism among juvenile offenders. By holding offenders accountable in a supportive environment and addressing the root causes of their behavior, RJ creates the conditions for long-term behavioral change.

- As RJ continues to expand, it could lead to lower overall crime rates and a more rehabilitative juvenile justice system.

Conclusion

Community and victim participation are essential elements of the Restorative Justice process, contributing to its overall success in reducing recidivism and fostering rehabilitation among juvenile offenders. Community involvement promotes accountability and provides a network of support for reintegration, while victim participation empowers victims to actively engage in the justice process, promoting healing and closure. Although there are challenges, such as the risk of stigmatization and retraumatization, the long-term benefits of community and victim participation in RJ are significant. As RJ becomes more widely adopted, its future impact will likely include stronger communities, a cultural shift toward restorative practices, and a more effective and humane juvenile justice system focused on rehabilitation rather than punishment.

CHAPTER 05

CHALLENGES AND LIMITAIONS OF RESTORATIVE JUSTICE IN JUVENILE SYSTEMS

5.1 Practical Limitations

While Restorative Justice (RJ) has demonstrated significant benefits in juvenile justice systems, several practical limitations hinder its full implementation and effectiveness. These challenges must be acknowledged and addressed to ensure RJ's continued success and expansion. This section outlines key limitations and provides suggestions on how these challenges can be resolved, especially in the interim, as RJ systems continue to evolve and adapt.

Inconsistency in Implementation Across Jurisdictions

One of the most significant limitations of RJ in juvenile justice is the inconsistent implementation across jurisdictions. While some regions have fully integrated RJ into their juvenile justice systems, others only use it sparingly or as a secondary option. This inconsistency can be attributed to a variety of factors, including differences in legal frameworks, resources, cultural attitudes toward punishment and rehabilitation, and the availability of trained RJ facilitators.

Challenges of Inconsistent Implementation:

- Unequal Access to RJ Programs: In jurisdictions where RJ is not fully integrated, juveniles may have limited access to restorative processes. This can result in unequal treatment, where some offenders benefit from RJ's rehabilitative approach, while others are subject to more punitive measures.

- Lack of Standardization: The absence of standardized RJ practices across different regions can lead to variability in outcomes. Some jurisdictions may apply RJ more effectively, while others may lack the resources or expertise to administer RJ programs that fully address the needs of offenders, victims, and the community.

- Resistance from Traditional Justice Systems: In some areas, legal professionals, judges, and policymakers may be resistant to adopting RJ, either due to unfamiliarity with the concept or a belief that punitive justice is more effective for maintaining law and order.

Possible Resolutions:

- National or Regional Frameworks for RJ: Governments should work toward establishing national or regional frameworks that standardize the implementation of RJ across all jurisdictions. These frameworks can provide clear guidelines for when and how RJ should be used in juvenile cases, ensuring that all offenders have access to restorative processes regardless of where they live.

- Training and Resources for Practitioners: Providing training programs for legal professionals, community volunteers, and RJ facilitators can help address the gap in knowledge and expertise. By equipping more people with the skills needed to run RJ programs, jurisdictions can expand the availability of restorative options and improve the quality of the outcomes.

- Pilot Programs in Under-Utilized Areas: Introducing pilot RJ programs in areas where RJ is underutilized can help demonstrate its effectiveness and build local support. Pilot programs can serve as a stepping stone toward broader implementation, allowing policymakers to assess the impact of RJ before committing to a more comprehensive adoption.

Appropriateness of RJ in Cases Involving Serious Crimes

Another key limitation of RJ is the debate over whether it is appropriate for addressing serious offenses, such as violent crimes, sexual offenses, or repeat offending. Critics argue that RJ may not provide an adequate response to these types of crimes, as the harm caused is more severe, and the potential for genuine reconciliation between the victim and offender may be limited. Moreover, there is concern that using RJ in these cases could result in lenient outcomes that fail to protect public safety or provide justice for the victim.

Challenges in Serious Crime Cases:

- Victim Trauma: In cases involving serious crimes, particularly violent or sexual offenses, the emotional trauma experienced by the victim may make it difficult or inappropriate for them to engage in a face-to-face dialogue with the offender. Victims may feel unsafe or pressured to forgive when they are not ready to do so.

- Public Perception of Leniency: The use of RJ in serious crime cases may be seen as a lenient response, particularly in societies where there is a strong demand for retributive justice. This perception can undermine public confidence in the justice system and lead to resistance against further expansion of RJ programs.

- Offender Accountability: There are concerns that RJ may not provide sufficient accountability for offenders in serious cases, particularly if the offender does not fully acknowledge their wrongdoing or fails to follow through on restitution agreements.

Possible Resolutions:

- Careful Case Selection: RJ should be used selectively in serious crime cases, ensuring that both the victim and offender are emotionally prepared for the process. Risk assessments and mental health evaluations should be conducted before proceeding with RJ to ensure that it is appropriate and beneficial for both parties.

- Hybrid Models of Justice: In cases of serious crimes, jurisdictions could consider using hybrid models that combine elements of both RJ and traditional justice. For example, RJ processes could be used to supplement, rather than replace, formal court proceedings. This allows victims to engage in dialogue and receive restitution while still ensuring that the offender faces legal consequences proportionate to the offense.

- Victim-Centered Safeguards: In cases involving serious trauma, additional safeguards should be put in place to protect the victim. For instance, indirect mediation (where the victim and offender do not meet face-to-face) or shuttle diplomacy (where a mediator communicates between the two parties) can be used to facilitate restorative outcomes without risking further harm to the victim.

Limited Resources and Funding

Many RJ programs struggle with limited resources and funding, which restricts their ability to operate effectively. Implementing RJ programs requires trained facilitators, mediators, support staff, and often specialized services such as counseling or therapy for both victims and offenders. In regions with underfunded justice systems, the resources required to sustain RJ programs may be scarce, resulting in inconsistent application or poorly managed processes.

Challenges of Resource Limitations:

- Insufficient Program Availability: Limited resources mean that RJ programs may only be available to a small number of juvenile offenders, leading to overburdened systems that cannot adequately meet the demand for restorative processes.

- Lack of Specialized Support Services: RJ requires specialized support services, such as counseling for victims and rehabilitation for offenders. In many areas, these services are not available, which can reduce the effectiveness of RJ programs in addressing the root causes of offending or supporting victim recovery.

- Volunteer Reliance: RJ programs often rely heavily on volunteers, which can lead to inconsistent quality. While volunteers play a crucial role in RJ, they may lack the professional expertise required for more complex or serious cases.

Possible Resolutions:

- Increased Government Funding: Governments should allocate increased funding to RJ programs, recognizing the long-term cost savings associated with reducing recidivism and improving rehabilitation outcomes. By investing in RJ, jurisdictions can reduce the burden on traditional court systems and detention centers.

- Public-Private Partnerships: Establishing public-private partnerships can help alleviate resource constraints. By partnering with non-governmental organizations (NGOs), community organizations, and private sector entities, governments can access additional resources and expertise to expand the reach of RJ programs.

- Building Capacity Through Training: To address the issue of limited expertise, governments and NGOs should provide comprehensive training programs for volunteers and facilitators. This can ensure that RJ processes are consistent and effective, even in regions with limited professional resources.

Resistance from Traditional Justice Systems

In some jurisdictions, there is resistance to RJ from traditional justice systems, including judges, prosecutors, and law enforcement officials. This resistance often stems from a belief that punitive justice is more effective in deterring crime, or from a lack of familiarity with RJ's principles and benefits. As a result, RJ may not be fully integrated into juvenile justice systems, or it may be viewed as a secondary option rather than a primary approach.

Challenges of Systemic Resistance:

- Reluctance to Divert Cases: Judges and prosecutors may be hesitant to divert cases to RJ processes, particularly if they are concerned about public safety or believe that punitive measures are necessary for deterrence.

- Institutional Inertia: Established legal systems may resist change due to institutional inertia, where traditional practices are maintained simply because they are familiar or entrenched in the system's structure.

- Lack of Awareness or Training: Many legal professionals may lack the awareness or training required to fully understand RJ's benefits. This can lead to misconceptions about the efficacy of RJ, particularly in terms of public safety and accountability.

Possible Resolutions:

- Education and Advocacy: One of the most effective ways to address resistance is through education and advocacy. Governments, NGOs, and RJ advocates should conduct outreach programs to educate legal professionals about the benefits of RJ, particularly in terms of reducing recidivism and promoting rehabilitation. Training programs for judges, prosecutors, and law enforcement can help build understanding and support for RJ.

- Demonstrating Results: Developing evidence-based pilot programs can help demonstrate the effectiveness of RJ in reducing recidivism and promoting victim satisfaction. By showcasing successful RJ outcomes, jurisdictions can build support within the traditional justice system.

- Gradual Integration: Rather than expecting immediate, full-scale adoption of RJ, policymakers should aim for gradual integration. Over time, as legal professionals become more familiar with RJ processes and see their benefits, resistance is likely to diminish.

Conclusion

While Restorative Justice offers many benefits, including reduced recidivism and improved rehabilitation outcomes for juveniles, it also faces several practical limitations. These include inconsistent implementation across jurisdictions, challenges in addressing serious crimes, limited resources, and resistance from traditional justice systems. To overcome these challenges in the interim, governments and communities must prioritize education, standardization, and increased funding for RJ programs. By addressing these limitations, RJ can be more fully integrated into juvenile justice systems, offering a more effective and humane alternative to punitive justice models.

5.2 Criticisms of Restorative Justice

While Restorative Justice (RJ) has gained traction as an alternative to punitive justice, it is not without its criticisms. Some argue that RJ is not always suitable for addressing certain types of crimes, particularly violent crimes and cases involving significant trauma. Critics claim that RJ may fail to meet the needs of victims who prefer a more punitive response, or who may not feel safe or satisfied by the outcomes of restorative processes. Additionally, there are concerns that RJ could be perceived as a "soft" approach that does not provide adequate deterrence for serious offenders, particularly in cases where the harm caused is severe.

Key Criticisms of RJ in Violent Crime Cases

1. Inadequate Addressing of Victim Needs in Violent Crimes:

- Critics argue that RJ may not always be the most appropriate response for victims of violent crimes, particularly when the trauma is severe. In these cases, victims may feel that facing their offender in a restorative setting is too overwhelming or emotionally damaging. They may prefer a more traditional justice approach, such as incarceration, that provides a clear punitive response to the harm caused.

- There is also concern that RJ may not adequately address the power dynamics involved in violent crimes, especially in cases of sexual violence, domestic abuse, or crimes where the offender holds significant power over the victim. In these situations, victims may feel pressured to participate in RJ processes or to forgive the offender before they are emotionally ready, leading to further victimization.

2. Perception of Leniency:

- Another common criticism is that RJ may be perceived as too lenient or as a "soft" option, particularly in cases involving violent or repeat offenders. Critics argue that without the threat of incarceration or other punitive measures, RJ may not provide a sufficient deterrent to future offending. This concern is heightened in cases of serious violent offenses, where the public or the victims may feel that justice is not adequately served through restorative measures alone.

- Some offenders, particularly in violent cases, may not engage in RJ processes in good faith, using the process as a way to avoid more severe legal consequences. If the offender does not show genuine remorse or take responsibility for their actions, RJ may fail to deliver the accountability necessary for both the victim and society.

3. Uneven Application in Violent Crime Cases:

- Critics also point to the uneven application of RJ in violent crime cases, where the outcomes may vary significantly depending on the offender, the victim, and the facilitator's skill. In some cases, RJ has failed to provide the necessary closure for victims, leaving them dissatisfied with the process. This lack of consistency, particularly in serious cases, can undermine the credibility of RJ and its perceived effectiveness.

Examples of RJ Failing to Address Violent Crimes Adequately

While there is evidence of RJ's success in many cases, there are notable examples where RJ has struggled to meet the needs of victims in violent crime cases, leading to criticism of its application in such contexts.

1. Case of Sexual Assault in the United Kingdom:

- In the United Kingdom, RJ was used in a case involving sexual assault where the victim, a young woman, participated in a restorative meeting with her attacker. While the process was voluntary, the victim later expressed dissatisfaction with the outcome, stating that she felt pressure to forgive her attacker, despite not feeling emotionally ready. The restorative meeting did not provide her with the closure or sense of justice she had hoped for.

- This case highlighted the potential risks of applying RJ in situations where victims are dealing with significant emotional trauma. Critics argue that in cases of sexual violence, RJ may not always be appropriate, as the emotional and psychological harm may require more formal therapeutic support and justice measures.

2. Domestic Violence Cases in Canada:

- In Canada, RJ has been applied in some cases of domestic violence, with mixed results. In several cases, victims reported feeling re-victimized during RJ processes, particularly when power imbalances between the victim and offender were not adequately addressed. Some victims expressed that the RJ process did not hold the offender accountable in a meaningful way, and they felt that the process was more focused on reconciliation than on their safety and well-being.

- Research from Canadian RJ programs has shown that, in certain domestic violence cases, victims felt pressured to reconcile or forgive, leading to further emotional harm. In cases where the offender showed little remorse or accountability, victims were left feeling unsupported and vulnerable. These cases point to the limitations of RJ in addressing crimes where the offender holds significant power over the victim, and where the risk of ongoing harm remains high.

3. Violent Crimes in South Africa:

- In South Africa, RJ has been used as part of the country's transition away from punitive apartheid-era policies toward more rehabilitative justice practices. While RJ has seen success in many areas, its application in violent crime cases, such as murder and assault, has faced significant criticism. In several high-profile cases, victims' families expressed dissatisfaction with the RJ process, arguing that it did not provide the level of justice or closure they desired.

- One such case involved a young offender who had committed a violent assault, and the victim's family participated in an RJ process. While the offender showed remorse and engaged in the process, the victim's family felt that the outcome—restitution and community service—was insufficient for the severity of the crime. This case illustrates the difficulty of applying RJ in serious violent crime cases, where the victims or their families may feel that the restorative outcome does not align with the gravity of the offense.

Challenges with RJ as a Deterrent in Serious Offenses

- Deterrence vs. Rehabilitation: One of the ongoing debates about RJ in serious offenses is whether RJ can effectively deter future crimes. Critics argue that without the threat of punitive measures, RJ may not be sufficient to deter serious repeat offenders. In contrast, RJ proponents argue that RJ focuses on long-term rehabilitation rather than short-term deterrence, but the perception of leniency in cases involving serious offenses remains a concern.

- Repeat Offenders: In some cases, RJ has been criticized for not being effective in dealing with repeat violent offenders. Offenders who do not fully engage in the restorative process or who manipulate the process to avoid harsher penalties may reoffend, leading to questions about RJ's ability to prevent future harm in cases where individuals have a history of violent behavior.

Addressing the Limitations:

To resolve the limitations of RJ in violent crime cases, several strategies could be considered:

1. Case-by-Case Basis: RJ should be applied selectively in cases involving violent crimes, ensuring that the victim is emotionally prepared and willing to participate. RJ should be optional in serious cases, with thorough risk assessments conducted beforehand.

2. Trauma-Informed Approach: RJ facilitators must be trained in trauma-informed practices to ensure that victims of violent crime receive the support they need throughout the process. Additional mental health resources, such as counseling and therapy, should be integrated into RJ programs for both victims and offenders.

3. Hybrid Models: In cases involving violent crimes, a hybrid approach that combines elements of RJ and traditional justice may be more appropriate. RJ can be used as a supplementary process, allowing for dialogue and restitution, while the formal justice system ensures that serious offenders face appropriate legal consequences.

4. Victim Safeguards: Additional safeguards should be put in place to protect victims in violent crime cases. These could include indirect mediation (where the victim does not meet face-to-face with the offender) or shuttle mediation (where a mediator communicates between the victim and offender without them meeting directly).

Conclusion

Restorative Justice has been criticized for its limitations, particularly in addressing the needs of victims in cases of violent crimes. The emotional and psychological trauma experienced by victims of such crimes may make RJ processes inadequate or even harmful if not handled properly. Critics argue that RJ's emphasis on dialogue and reconciliation can sometimes feel too lenient, particularly in cases where the harm caused is severe. Despite these challenges, RJ remains a valuable tool for promoting healing and accountability, though it must be applied selectively and with appropriate safeguards in place for serious offenses. By adopting a case-by-case approach and ensuring trauma-informed practices, RJ can continue to offer a meaningful alternative to traditional punitive justice, even in the most challenging cases.

5.3 Resource and Training Constraints

One of the most significant challenges to the widespread implementation of Restorative Justice (RJ) in juvenile justice systems is the resource and training constraints faced by many jurisdictions. RJ is a labor-intensive process that requires a well-developed infrastructure, including trained facilitators, mediators, and comprehensive support systems for both victims and offenders. However, many juvenile justice systems, particularly in underfunded or overburdened regions, lack the financial and organizational resources needed to implement RJ effectively on a broad scale. These constraints limit the accessibility and quality of RJ programs, undermining their potential to serve as an alternative to traditional punitive justice.

Key Resource and Training Constraints in Implementing Restorative Justice

1. Lack of Trained RJ Facilitators and Mediators

- RJ processes, such as Victim-Offender Mediation (VOM), Family Group Conferencing (FGC), and Restorative Circles, require highly skilled facilitators and mediators to guide the restorative process effectively. These professionals must be able to navigate complex emotional dynamics, ensure the safety and well-being of participants, and create an environment conducive to dialogue, accountability, and healing.

- However, many regions lack sufficient numbers of trained RJ practitioners. In some cases, RJ programs rely on volunteers or under-trained staff, which can lead to inconsistent outcomes or even re-traumatization of participants, particularly in cases involving severe harm or trauma.

2. Insufficient Funding and Budgetary Constraints

- Implementing RJ programs requires substantial financial investment. Funding is needed for staff salaries, program materials, facilities, and ongoing support services for victims and offenders, such as counseling, rehabilitation, and reintegration assistance. However, many juvenile justice systems are underfunded, particularly in regions where the criminal justice system is already overburdened or facing resource shortages.

- In low-resource settings, RJ programs may struggle to secure sustainable funding, limiting their reach and effectiveness. Without adequate funding, RJ programs may be forced to cut back on essential services, such as ongoing victim support, post-restitution monitoring, or professional development for RJ facilitators.

3. Lack of Comprehensive Support Systems

- RJ is not a stand-alone process; it requires the integration of support systems that address the needs of both victims and offenders. Victims often require psychological counseling, trauma support, and practical assistance in rebuilding their lives, while offenders need access to educational, vocational, and therapeutic services to support their rehabilitation.

- In many jurisdictions, particularly in under-resourced areas, these support systems are either underdeveloped or non-existent. Without access to these services, the success of RJ programs is limited, as the underlying issues that contribute to criminal behavior (such as poverty, family dysfunction, or substance abuse) remain unaddressed.

4. Regional Disparities in RJ Infrastructure

- RJ implementation varies significantly across regions. While some jurisdictions have developed comprehensive RJ programs with dedicated funding, staff, and support structures, others have only rudimentary or pilot programs in place. These disparities lead to unequal access to RJ, where some juveniles benefit from restorative processes while others are forced into traditional punitive systems.

- In some areas, RJ may only be available to juveniles who commit minor offenses, while more serious cases are excluded due to a lack of capacity to handle complex or high-risk situations.

Addressing Resource and Training Constraints

While resource and training constraints present significant challenges, there are several strategies that juvenile justice systems can adopt to mitigate these issues and support the broader implementation of RJ. These approaches involve increasing investment, improving training programs, leveraging community resources, and creating innovative models of RJ delivery that can function in low-resource settings.

1. Increasing Investment in Restorative Justice Programs

Governments and local authorities must recognize the long-term benefits of RJ, including reducing recidivism, improving rehabilitation outcomes, and alleviating the burden on courts and detention centers. By investing in RJ, jurisdictions can reduce the overall costs associated with punitive justice, such as incarceration and legal expenses. Governments can allocate specific funding for:

- Training Programs for RJ Facilitators: Developing comprehensive training programs for RJ practitioners is essential to ensure that mediators and facilitators have the skills necessary to navigate complex cases effectively. Governments and NGOs can collaborate to provide certification programs for RJ professionals, ensuring a high standard of practice across regions.

- Victim and Offender Support Services: Funding should also be directed toward creating and maintaining support systems for both victims and offenders, such as counseling, mental health services, and educational opportunities. These services are critical for addressing the root causes of offending and supporting long-term rehabilitation.

2. Leveraging Community Resources

In many jurisdictions, particularly in lower-income regions, RJ programs can benefit from community involvement. By leveraging community resources, governments can reduce the financial burden of RJ programs and increase their reach. Community volunteers, local organizations, and NGOs can provide:

- Voluntary Mediation and Facilitation: While volunteers should receive professional training, community members can play an important role as RJ mediators and facilitators. Community-led initiatives can create a more localized approach to RJ, where mediators understand the specific cultural and social contexts of the offender and victim.

- Community Support Networks: Communities can offer support networks for both offenders and victims by providing mentorship, rehabilitation services, and opportunities for reintegration, such as employment or education.

3. Innovative RJ Models for Low-Resource Settings

Jurisdictions facing severe resource constraints can explore innovative RJ models that are designed to function in low-resource settings. These models focus on flexibility, efficiency, and maximizing existing resources. Examples include:

- Virtual Restorative Circles: For regions that cannot afford physical facilities for RJ meetings, virtual RJ processes can be implemented using technology. While face-to-face interaction is ideal, virtual meetings can still facilitate meaningful dialogue between victims and offenders, especially in areas with logistical or financial limitations.

- School-Based RJ Programs: Schools are an ideal setting for RJ, particularly for addressing juvenile offenses that occur within educational environments. School-based RJ programs can reduce the need for court involvement in minor cases and serve as an early intervention tool to prevent future criminal behavior.

4. Collaboration with NGOs and International Organizations

NGOs and international organizations play a critical role in supporting RJ programs, particularly in developing regions or jurisdictions facing financial constraints. By collaborating with these organizations, governments can access additional resources, expertise, and training opportunities. Key areas for collaboration include:

- Capacity Building: NGOs can provide capacity-building programs for local justice systems, helping to establish RJ infrastructure and train facilitators in best practices.

- Research and Evaluation: Partnering with universities and research institutions can help jurisdictions evaluate the success of their RJ programs and make data-driven decisions about expanding or improving these initiatives.

Future Outlook

Addressing resource and training constraints is essential to expanding RJ's reach and effectiveness in juvenile justice systems. While these challenges may limit the full-scale implementation of RJ in the short term, strategic investments in training, infrastructure, and community involvement can gradually build the capacity needed for RJ to become a primary approach to juvenile justice. In the long term, increased funding and greater collaboration between governments, NGOs, and community organizations will create a more sustainable model for RJ, ensuring that all juveniles have access to restorative processes that promote rehabilitation and reintegration.

By overcoming these constraints, jurisdictions can maximize the potential of RJ to transform the juvenile justice system into one that prioritizes healing, accountability, and community engagement over punishment.

CHAPTER 06

CONCLUSION AND POLICY RECOMMENDATIONS

6.1 Conclusion

Restorative Justice (RJ) represents a transformative shift in how juvenile crime is addressed, offering a more holistic and rehabilitative approach compared to traditional punitive systems. By focusing on healing, accountability, and community involvement, RJ addresses not only the behavior of the offender but also the needs of victims and the broader community. The evidence from various jurisdictions around the world clearly shows that RJ can reduce recidivism, promote rehabilitation, and improve victim satisfaction, making it a viable and often superior alternative to retributive justice for juveniles.

RJ's emphasis on personal growth, empathy development, and reparation provides young offenders with the opportunity to understand the impact of their actions, take responsibility, and reintegrate into society as productive members. Unlike punitive approaches that isolate and stigmatize offenders, RJ offers pathways for healing, both for offenders and victims, by fostering dialogue and collaborative problem-solving.

However, the implementation of RJ is not without challenges. Inconsistent application across regions, resource and training constraints, and concerns about the appropriateness of RJ for serious crimes have raised questions about its scalability and universal applicability. Nonetheless, these challenges can be addressed through strategic investments, tailored approaches to serious offenses, and increased training for RJ practitioners.

In conclusion, RJ offers a promising alternative to traditional juvenile justice systems, focusing on long-term rehabilitation and societal reintegration rather than punishment. When implemented effectively, RJ can significantly improve outcomes for young offenders, victims, and the community, making it a model that aligns with both justice and human development.

6.2 Policy Recommendations

To fully realize the potential of Restorative Justice in juvenile systems, several policy recommendations must be considered. These recommendations focus on expanding access to RJ, improving the quality of RJ processes, and ensuring that RJ is applied consistently and appropriately across different regions and cases.

1. Standardization of RJ Practices Across Jurisdictions

- Recommendation: Governments should work toward creating national or regional frameworks that standardize RJ practices. This will ensure that RJ is consistently applied across all jurisdictions, giving every juvenile offender the opportunity to benefit from restorative processes.

- Implementation Strategy: Develop national guidelines and best practices for RJ, and provide funding to local governments to establish RJ programs in under-served areas. This could include creating specialized RJ units within juvenile justice systems to oversee the implementation and ensure compliance with national standards.

2. Increased Investment in RJ Programs and Support Services

- Recommendation: Governments and local authorities should allocate more resources to RJ programs, with a particular focus on training facilitators, mediators, and support staff. Victim and offender support services, such as counseling and rehabilitation, should be integrated into RJ processes to ensure comprehensive care for all participants.

- Implementation Strategy: Prioritize funding for RJ training programs, build partnerships with NGOs and international organizations, and establish sustainable financing mechanisms (such as public-private partnerships) to expand RJ availability.

3. Case-by-Case Application of RJ for Serious Crimes

- Recommendation: RJ should be applied carefully in cases involving serious crimes, with a focus on voluntary participation by victims and offenders. A hybrid model that combines RJ with traditional justice processes may be more appropriate for serious offenses, ensuring accountability while still providing opportunities for dialogue and restitution.

- Implementation Strategy: Establish clear guidelines for when and how RJ should be used in serious crime cases, ensuring that all stakeholders (including victims, offenders, and legal professionals) are fully informed and supported.

This may include offering trauma-informed mediation services and providing additional safeguards to protect victims.

4. Expansion of School-Based RJ Programs

- Recommendation: School-based RJ programs should be expanded as part of broader efforts to prevent juvenile crime and address conflicts early. Schools offer an ideal setting for early intervention, helping juveniles learn conflict resolution skills and avoid escalation into the criminal justice system.

- Implementation Strategy: Allocate funding for the integration of RJ programs into schools, train school staff in RJ practices, and develop partnerships with local community organizations to support these initiatives.

5. Enhanced Training for RJ Practitioners and Volunteers

- Recommendation: RJ practitioners, including mediators and facilitators, must receive comprehensive training to handle the emotional and logistical complexities of RJ processes. Special attention should be given to training in trauma-informed care and culturally sensitive practices.

- Implementation Strategy: Develop accredited training programs for RJ practitioners, with a focus on best practices for working with juveniles and victims of serious crimes. Provide ongoing professional development opportunities to ensure that practitioners remain skilled and adaptable to new challenges.

6. Monitoring and Evaluation of RJ Programs

- Recommendation: Governments should establish mechanisms for monitoring and evaluating the effectiveness of RJ programs to ensure they are achieving the desired outcomes of reducing recidivism, promoting rehabilitation, and supporting victims.

- Implementation Strategy: Create a system of regular data collection and analysis to assess the success of RJ programs. Partner with academic institutions and research organizations to evaluate RJ outcomes and identify areas for improvement.

7. Public Education and Awareness Campaigns

- Recommendation: Public education campaigns should be launched to raise awareness about the benefits of RJ, particularly in communities where there is resistance to non-punitive justice models. Educating the public about RJ can help to build trust and support for restorative practices.

- Implementation Strategy: Develop media campaigns, community workshops, and informational resources to promote RJ and explain how it benefits victims, offenders, and society at large. Engage community leaders and local organizations to act as RJ advocates.

Conclusion

The success of Restorative Justice in juvenile systems depends on thoughtful implementation, sustained investment, and a commitment to addressing challenges as they arise. By standardizing RJ practices, increasing resources, and ensuring that RJ is applied appropriately in serious cases, juvenile justice systems can transform into models of rehabilitation and reintegration. With these policy recommendations, RJ can continue to evolve as a powerful tool for promoting accountability, healing, and long-term change for juvenile offenders and their communities.

CHAPTER 07

REFERENCES

Here are suggested references from academic journals, books, and other sources relevant to Restorative Justice in juvenile justice systems. These references cover theoretical foundations, case studies, empirical data, and practical applications.

Books

- Zehr, H. (2002). The Little Book of Restorative Justice. Intercourse, PA: Good Books.

- This book offers a concise introduction to the principles and practices of Restorative Justice, with an emphasis on its application in both adult and juvenile justice systems.

- Johnstone, G., & Van Ness, D. W. (Eds.) (2007). Handbook of Restorative Justice. Cullompton: Willan Publishing.

- This comprehensive handbook provides a global overview of Restorative Justice, including its theoretical foundations and application in juvenile justice systems.

- Morris, A., & Maxwell, G. (Eds.) (2001). Restorative Justice for Juveniles: Conferencing, Mediation and Circles. Oxford: Hart Publishing.

- This book offers insights into various Restorative Justice models, including Family Group Conferencing and Victim-Offender Mediation, with specific reference to their use in juvenile justice.

Journal Articles

- McCold, P., & Wachtel, B. (2003). "In Pursuit of Paradigm: A Theory of Restorative Justice." Restorative Justice: Theoretical Foundations, 5(1), 21-40.

- This article presents a theoretical model for Restorative Justice, including a focus on how it applies to juvenile offenders and promotes rehabilitation.

- Bazemore, G., & Umbreit, M. (2001). "A Comparison of Four Restorative Conferencing Models." Juvenile Justice Bulletin, U.S. Department of Justice.

- This bulletin compares different restorative conferencing models, such as Family Group Conferencing and Victim-Offender Mediation, with data on their effectiveness in juvenile cases.

- Nugent, W. R., Umbreit, M. S., Wiinamaki, L., & Paddock, J. (2001). "Participation in Victim-Offender Mediation and the Prevalence of Subsequent Delinquent Behavior: A Meta-Analysis." Research on Social Work Practice, 11(4), 463-478.

- This meta-analysis reviews the impact of Victim-Offender Mediation on reducing recidivism rates among juvenile offenders, providing empirical data on its effectiveness.

- Rodriguez, N. (2007). "Restorative Justice at Work: Examining the Impact of Restorative Justice on Juvenile Recidivism." Crime & Delinquency, 53(3), 355-379.

- This article examines the outcomes of Restorative Justice programs, specifically focusing on their impact on reducing recidivism rates among juveniles.

- Hayes, H., & Daly, K. (2004). "Conferencing and Re-offending in Queensland." Australian & New Zealand Journal of Criminology, 37(2), 167-191.

- This research article explores the effectiveness of conferencing as a Restorative Justice practice in juvenile justice systems in Queensland, Australia.

Reports and Policy Papers

- Shapland, J., Robinson, G., & Sorsby, A. (2011). Restorative Justice in Practice: Evaluating What Works for Victims and Offenders. Routledge.

- This report provides an evaluation of RJ practices, with a focus on the experiences of both victims and juvenile offenders. It includes empirical data and policy recommendations.

- Ministry of Justice (New Zealand). (2018). Youth Justice Indicators Summary Report.

- This government report details the implementation and outcomes of New Zealand's Family Group Conferencing model in juvenile justice, focusing on recidivism rates and youth rehabilitation.

- Center for Juvenile Justice Reform (CJJR). (2019). Restorative Justice: A Positive Youth Development Approach.

- This policy paper explores how Restorative Justice aligns with positive youth development and suggests strategies for integrating RJ into juvenile justice systems in the United States.

Case Studies

- Maxwell, G., & Morris, A. (2006). "Youth Justice in New Zealand: Restorative Practices in an International Context." Youth Justice, 6(2), 107-117.

- This case study highlights New Zealand's successful integration of Restorative Justice practices into its juvenile justice system through the Family Group Conferencing model.

- Umbreit, M. S., Coates, R. B., & Vos, B. (2004). "Victim-Offender Mediation: Three Decades of Practice and Research." Conflict Resolution Quarterly, 22(1), 279-303.

- This article provides a comprehensive review of Victim-Offender Mediation as a Restorative Justice practice, with a focus on juvenile offenders in various countries.